chicken

other idg cookbooks by paulette mitchell:

The 15-Minute Gourmet: Vegetarian

The 15-Minute Gourmet: Noodles

The 15-Minute Single Gourmet

The Complete Book of Dressings

The Complete Soy Cookbook

chicken

paulette mitchell

IDG BOOKS WORLDWIDE

AN INTERNATIONAL DATA GROUP COMPANY

Foster City, CA • Chicago, IL • Indianapolis, IN • New York, NY • Southlake, TX

IDG Books Worldwide, Inc.
An International Data Group Company
919 East Hillsdale Boulevard
Suite 400
Foster City, CA 94404

The IDG Books Worldwide logo is a registered trademark under the exclusive license to IDG Books Worldwide, Inc., from International Data Group, Inc.

For general information on IDG Books Worldwide's books in the U.S., please call our Consumer Customer Service department at 800-762-2974. For reseller information including discounts and premium sales, please call our Reseller Customer Service department at 800-434-3422.

Library of Congress Cataloging-in-Publication Data
Mitchell, Paulette
        The 15-minute gourmet: chicken / by Paulette Mitchell.
                p.   cm. — (15-minute gourmet)
        New ed. of: The 15-minute chicken gourmet / Paulette
        Mitchell. c1997
        ISBN 0-02-863279-6 (alk. paper)
        1. Cookery (chicken) 2. Quick and easy cookery. I. Mitchell,
        Paulette. 15-minute chicken gourmet. II. Title. III. Title:
        Fifteen-minute gourmet. IV. Series.
TX750.5.C45M58   1999
641.6'65—dc21   99-39848
                                                          CIP

Manufactured in the United States of America
10   9   8   7   6   5   4   3

Interior and cover design by Scott Meola
Cover photo by Nora Scarlett
Clock image © 1995 Chris Collins/The Stock Market
Silverware image © 1999 Photodisc
Cover photo: Chicken Kabobs with Tomato-Soy Marinade, page 89

To Aunt Annie, with thanks and appreciation, for inspiring me at age 7 with my first cooking lessons, and to my students for inspiring me to begin writing cookbooks.

acknowledgments

Special thanks to Cindy Jurgensen, my friend and cooking assistant; to Justin Schwartz and Linda Ingroia, my editors at IDG; and to Jane Dystel, my agent. Thank you also to production editor Arun Das, designer Scott Meola, photographer Nora Scarlett, and food stylist Dolores Custer and her assistants Lisa Homa and Judi Orlick.

contents

introduction

THROUGHOUT THE CENTURIES, CHICKEN HAS PLAYED A

starring role in many of the world's cuisines. And here at

home, as more and more Americans are making a con-

scious decision to eat less and less red meat, chicken

consumption is on the rise. In fact, statistics show that

chicken is now eaten in most American households at

least once a week.

As for me, once I accepted my editor's challenge to develop 100 quick-to-prepare chicken recipes, the versatility of chicken took on a new meaning for me. Creating the recipes and preparing each of them two, three, or four times after their inception meant a lot of chicken! My family and I feasted on chicken night after night. I discovered the possibilities to be unlimited, and dinner never failed to be a culinary adventure.

Chicken decidedly has become the meat of choice for health- and taste-conscious consumers. Chicken is often the best choice for serving guests. And it's no coincidence. No other meat can be cooked in as many interesting ways. The mild flavor of chicken is compatible with an almost endless variety of herbs and spices, fruits and vegetables. Chicken can be enjoyed hot, at room temperature, or chilled. You can serve chicken with pasta, chicken with rice, chicken with fruit or vegetables, chicken with wine, chicken salads, and the ultimate comfort food, chicken soup.

Today's cooks not only want food that tastes good—they also want food that is healthful. Chicken can be cooked with little or no fat. My chicken recipes address this issue, an important food-related health concern. The recipes also reflect the growing fascination with ethnic influences and emphasize cooking with fresh foods, beans, grains, and pasta.

The popularity of my 15-minute cookbooks and my 15-minute cooking classes has confirmed the need for a wide variety of gourmet recipes that can be prepared quickly. Cooking with chicken is a natural for the 15-minute concept; it's one of the best ways to have a complete, nutritious, and delicious meal on the table fast. Chopped or diced, chicken can be sautéed or stir-fried in about 5 minutes; skinless, boneless chicken breast halves take no more than 10 minutes to grill or broil.

Fifteen-minute recipes rely on the imaginative use of fresh ingredients rather than elaborate techniques. I have adapted several classic chicken dishes to lower-fat ingredients and quicker cooking methods; other recipes combine supermarket ingredients in out-of-the-ordinary ways.

Fast meals are simplified meals. Many of these chicken dishes need only the accompaniment of a salad and warm, crusty bread; others simply call for the addition of pasta or rice. In celebration of the versatility of chicken, you'll find dishes to suit every occasion. There are recipes for serving your family on busy weeknights, like Chicken Fajitas (page 10) or Chicken Noodle Soup (page 164). Others will delight your most discriminating guests, like Chicken Marsala on Egg Noodles (page 54) or Walnut Chicken with Sherry Sauce (page 20). And each dish delivers variety, speed, and first-rate flavor.

Because my recipes are simple and easy to follow, this book appeals to novices. Yet it is sophisticated enough to satisfy experienced cooks and demanding diners. You will not spend a great deal of time cooking—but no one need ever know it. Using fresh, flavorful ingredients and the game plan provided, you will achieve amazing results with minimum effort—guaranteed.

Ingredients for 15-Minute Chicken

Since these recipes are based primarily on using fresh ingredients—fresh vegetables, fresh fruits, and fresh chicken—begin by planning your trip to the supermarket. Read your recipe and select your garnishes and accompaniments; look at the suggested variations (or come up with your own) in order to make the most of in-season produce.

While shopping, keep in mind that one of the keys to 15-minute success is purchasing top quality ingredients; this becomes especially important when the number of ingredients is minimal or when they are served uncooked. Whenever possible, select fully ripe produce. As a time-saver, some vegetables can be purchased chopped, such as broccoli and cauliflower florets and sliced mushrooms. Buy fresh herbs whenever possible (or grow them yourself). In addition, some canned and frozen foods are certainly helpful and acceptable; I purchase canned tomatoes, beans, and chicken broth and frozen corn and peas. Always keep on hand a variety of vinegars, olive oil, low-sodium soy sauce, and an assortment of pastas and rices.

The process of disjointing and deboning whole chickens can be daunting and time-consuming. Fortunately, boneless, skinless chicken breasts are readily available at nearly all supermarkets, day in, day out, all year long. They prove to be an appealing basis for the recipes in this book because they are mild in flavor, tender, and juicy. Lower in saturated fat than most other meats, a 4-ounce serving, when cooked using a low-fat method, contains only 170 calories—plus it is exceedingly low in fat, only 3 grams, while providing 33 grams of high-quality protein. The amount of protein per calorie makes chicken the most efficient protein source of all meats.

Some people think chicken is moister if cooked with the skin on; they then remove the skin just before eating. However, in developing my quickly prepared recipes with sauces and marinades, I have found skinless breasts to be moist and delicious—in addition to being lower in fat. Plus, if the skin is discarded after cooking, some of the seasonings go with it.

Compared to bone-in chicken breasts, the boneless, skinless ones cook much more quickly—another bonus for the 15-minute cook. If the meat is slightly flattened or cut into cubes, chunks, or strips, the chicken can cook in about 5 minutes, allowing time to create ethnic dishes that incorporate vegetables and other foods.

A quick lesson in terminology: A whole chicken breast is two breast halves joined in the center by cartilage. When sold skinless and boneless, each piece is actually a half breast, weighing 3 to 5 ounces. When you look closely, each of these halves consists of a large piece and a small fillet. These fillets, sold in packages labeled "chicken tenders," are sometimes a wise choice, because the small tender pieces are excellent in stir-fries and some salads. Other chicken packages are labeled "extra juicy." Checking the small print, you will see that these boneless, skinless chicken breast halves have been marinated in a flavorless liquid tenderizer. This usually yields a more tender end product, and does not affect the flavors when used in recipes.

In my recipes, I usually suggest 4 ounces per serving if the breasts are to be served alone, as in marinated and broiled chicken breasts; the ingredient lists specify the number of chicken breast halves. In recipes where the breasts are to be cut into pieces, as in stir-fries and braised dishes, the amount of chicken is listed by ounces. Three ounces per serving is usually just right when the recipe incorporates numerous other ingredients such as vegetables or pasta. Of course, the per-serving amount of chicken can be increased or decreased to suit your taste.

In my chicken cooking classes, I am frequently asked if the benefits of buying free-range or organic chickens outweigh the extra cost over mass-produced chickens. A "free-range" chicken is, supposedly, one that has roamed and foraged for food in a barnyard, as opposed to chickens that are raised in coops. These barnyard chickens can be very tasty; they can also be thin, tough, and "gamier" in flavor. If your goal is to avoid chemicals and growth hormones, look for "organic" chickens. They are not necessarily free-range chickens, but instead are raised on small poultry farms. Mass-produced chickens are sometimes raised with chemicals and antibiotics; other commercial growers promote their chickens by saying they have been fed only top-quality grains and were given no growth hormones. Many of these are tasteful and consistently tender. Free-range and organic chickens are most often found in gourmet markets, natural-food stores, or specialty meat markets; some diners swear they taste better. Give mass-produced, free-range, and organic chickens a try, and make a decision based on your own taste test.

Whichever type of fresh chicken you select, look for moist, unblemished, plump, and firm parts. Optimum freshness is all-important. Always check the "sell by" or "use by" date printed on the package. I patronize a busy market with a high turnover and high overall standards. Nevertheless, I try to purchase chicken the day I plan to cook it, and never more than 2 days in advance. The chicken will remain fresh for this length of time if it is properly handled.

Fresh chicken which has never been frozen is a better choice than parts which have been frozen; in my opinion, frozen chicken usually is lacking in flavor. If frozen, however, make sure the chicken is rock-hard and that it has not been frozen for more than 2 months. The wrapping must be intact to prevent freezer burn and ice crystals. Pinkish-colored ice in the package is a sign that the chicken has been at least partially defrosted and refrozen. This does not mean the chicken is spoiled, but the taste may suffer.

Even though I much prefer using fresh chicken, I always keep a pound of boneless, skinless chicken breast halves in the freezer. Several recipes, such as Chicken with Linguine and Tomato-Basil Sauce (page 59) and Curried Chicken and Rice Soup (page 169), can be made by pairing the thawed chicken with pantry staples when I don't have time to run to the store.

Chicken Safety

Fresh chicken is highly perishable and must be handled and cooked properly. Salmonella is one of the numerous bacteria that can infect chickens and eggs, as well as many other foods. Salmonella can be deadly, but avoiding it and other bacteria in chicken is quite simple. Just follow these guidelines:

- Bring chicken directly home from the market, especially in warm weather.

- Keep fresh chicken in the coldest part of your refrigerator, no longer than 2 days from the time of purchase to cooking. Leave the plastic wrapping intact to prevent moisture loss; butcher paper, however, should be replaced with plastic wrap or sealed plastic storage bags. Place the package on a dish so that juices cannot drip onto other foods. (If repackaging is necessary, wash the chicken under cold running water, then pat it dry with paper towels to reduce the bacteria that grow in moisture.)

- If chicken breasts cannot be used within 2 days, freeze them. Remove them from the store wrappings, wash and pat dry with paper towels. Then tightly wrap them in freezer paper or aluminum foil. Or, if you prefer, freeze the chicken in an airtight container.

- If you are using frozen chicken, gradual thawing in the refrigerator (24 hours maximum) is recommended to preserve quality. Be sure to place the wrapped chicken on a plate to catch the drippings as it defrosts. If you're in a hurry, place the wrapped chicken in a large bowl of cold water; this cuts thawing time in half. Most important: Do not leave chicken out to thaw at room temperature. Cook the chicken soon after defrosting (to guarantee even cooking throughout, be certain the chicken is thoroughly thawed prior to cooking) and do not refreeze it. Use a microwave for thawing only if you plan to cook the chicken immediately. Personally, I prefer not to thaw chicken in the microwave; too often, the thin edges begin to cook.

- Marinate chicken in the refrigerator, not at room temperature. (See page 61 for more details on marinating.)

- The greatest risk for salmonella contamination—more than in storing or cooking—is careless cleaning of kitchen surfaces and tools. When you are ready to cook the chicken, rinse it with cool water and pat it dry with paper towels. Immediately after use, use hot, soapy water to wash all work surfaces, plates that held the raw chicken, knives, shears, and your hands. You may even want to use a brush under your nails. Since salmonella can easily be transferred to other foods, never let the raw meat or juices from the meat touch other foods, especially those that are to be eaten uncooked. Most authorities caution against using wooden cutting boards, which are more likely to harbor bacteria; acrylic boards are preferable. I usually use poultry shears to cut chicken, avoiding the use of a cutting board altogether.

- Thorough cooking will destroy any bacteria; poultry cooked to an internal temperature of 180°F is safe. Since boneless, skinless chicken breast halves are thin, using a meat thermometer is unrealistic. Instead, test cooked chicken at the thickest part. Properly cooked chicken breasts will be white throughout, with no traces of pink; the juices will run clear rather than red when pricked with a knife point, and the texture will be fork-tender. Unlike red meat, chicken should never be served rare; do not even taste raw or partially cooked chicken. But don't overdo it either; overcooked chicken loses its wonderful flavor and tender texture—instead, it turns dry and leathery.

- Always put cooked chicken on a clean platter, not the one that held the raw chicken.

- Leftover cooked chicken should not be left at room temperature; refrigerate it as soon as possible. Cooked chicken dishes can be refrigerated for 1 or 2 days. Frozen, they will keep for up to 2 weeks, if packaged in an airtight container.

- If in doubt, throw it out. The bacteria that cause foodborne illnesses do not necessarily look, taste, or smell spoiled.

Cooking Methods for the 15-Minute Cook

The way chicken is prepared is an important factor in determining its healthfulness because some cooking methods can turn chicken into a high-fat food. Battered and fried with the skin on, a 4-ounce serving will contain 295 calories and 15 grams of fat. The same 4-ounce serving with no skin, prepared with a low-fat cooking method, contains 170 calories with 3 grams of fat.

Since bold, full-bodied flavors can be achieved with herbs and spices, fruits and vegetables, and marinades and sauces, low-fat cooking methods provide successful ways to enjoy chicken. Personally, I like to use a variety of cooking procedures during the week (as well as dishes from a variety of cuisines): sautéing, stir-frying, broiling, baking, stovetop and outdoor grilling, poaching, and cooking in soup broth. In some cases, the recipes' methods are interchangeable; this information is included in the Variations to the recipes. Microwaving has been eliminated because, in my opinion, the results are often inferior and the time saved is minimal; also, the methods I have used help you avoid overcooking. But I sometimes use my microwave for reheating leftovers, especially soups; and it offers a quick way to steam vegetables to be incorporated into recipes or used as an accompaniment.

Always rinse chicken with cool water and pat it dry with paper towels after you remove it from the package. Using poultry shears or a sharp paring knife, trim visible fat and the tough white tendon under the fillet. If you are cooking several chicken breasts that vary in thickness, the thicker pieces can be slightly flattened (see Tip, page xviii). Flattened chicken will cook more evenly. The pressing or pounding of the flattening procedure also helps tenderize the chicken by breaking down some of the fibers. In some supermarkets, you will find ready-to-use chicken breast fillets.

When cutting up a chicken breast, the size and shape of the pieces varies by the recipe. For visual appeal, the primary ingredients of a dish should be compatible in size and shape. Cutting chicken into bite-size pieces (such as for stir-fries or soups) is easier if the fresh chicken is placed in the freezer for an hour or so; the slightly frozen texture makes it much easier to make clean, smooth cuts. (If the meat is already frozen, transfer it from the freezer to the refrigerator in the morning; by evening, the not-quite-thawed texture should be ideal for slicing.) It is best to allow the chicken to thaw before cooking—but with small pieces this won't take long. For time savings, use the precut chicken available in some markets. It is usually labeled "chicken for stir-frying." (Check the label to be certain the chicken pieces are unseasoned.)

I'm sometimes asked if these chicken dishes or their leftovers freeze well. Quite honestly, I do not recommend this practice. The quality and texture of foods nearly always deteriorate after being frozen and thawed, which diminishes the benefits of using flavorful, fresh ingredients. If delicious, nutritious, fresh food can be made in just 15 minutes, why freeze? And the leftovers, if you have any, can be refrigerated for serving the next day.

Equipment for the 15-Minute Recipes

You do not need a lot of elaborate equipment for 15-minute cooking, nor do you need a large kitchen. However, a careful selection of equipment will not only speed up the process but will also add to your enjoyment of cooking. Buy the best quality you can afford—especially when it comes to pots, pans, and knives. As you use my 15-minute recipes, you will see that they were planned to simplify cleanup as well as cooking. Most recipes require only one or two pans.

My favorite pans are heavy-duty and have nonstick surfaces; they were used in developing these recipes. The weight and quality of nonstick pans is as important as their lining; thin pans do not distribute heat evenly. Today's nonstick pans have a permanent finish that reduces the amount of oil needed and also speeds cleanup. If you treat these top-quality tools of the trade carefully (never placing them over high heat—medium-high maximum—and using nonabrasive utensils for cooking and cleaning), they should last a lifetime.

For sautéed and stir-fried recipes yielding 4 servings, I most often use a large (10- or 12-inch) skillet with low, sloped sides. Because braising requires added liquid, it is best done in a 12-inch sauté pan with straight rather than sloped sides; a tight-fitting lid is important for the simmering stage of the procedure. A medium-size sauté pan with a lid can be used for poaching chicken. For cooking pasta, I suggest a pasta pot with a built-in colander. For soups, I use a Dutch oven or a large saucepan with a lid. And rice is best prepared in a rice cooker, although a large, heavy saucepan with a tight-fitting lid will do. Sauces can be made in a small or medium-size saucepan. A stovetop grill pan (preferably nonstick) is my choice for cooking marinated chicken breasts and chicken for composed salads. I use a food processor for grating and puréeing. Most of my chopping is done with my chef's knife; a smaller knife is suitable for some of the smaller tasks. A set of graduated stainless steel bowls, a nonstick baking sheet, poultry shears, ladles, spatulas, tongs, measuring spoons, measuring cups (for both liquid and dry ingredients), whisks and spoons for stirring, and, of course, a timer: That's about it for the necessities.

15-Minute Success

Once you have taken stock of your equipment and made your trip to the supermarket, you're ready to feast on short notice!

For 15-minute cooking efficiency, begin by reading over the recipe. Take note:

- Many of the recipes have less fat than their traditional versions. I use primarily olive oil and canola or safflower oil, depending on the other flavors in the recipes. The amount is based upon the use of nonstick cookware; to lower the fat content even further, nonstick cooking spray can be substituted. Low-fat versions of dairy products such as yogurt and sour cream have proved successful in these recipes.

- Vegetables are fresh unless specified otherwise. Frozen corn and peas are more practical for the 15-minute cook, since using fresh is quite time-consuming.

- Some ingredients, such as curry powder, red pepper flakes, pepper, and hot pepper sauce are followed by the words "or to taste"; these hot-flavored seasonings should be adjusted to suit your personal preference. Always taste the food and adjust the seasonings before serving.

- Quantities are provided for herbs in both their dried and fresh forms, where applicable; fresh herbs may need to be added later in the cooking procedure as specified.

- Little or no salt is called for in these recipes; this may be a matter of personal taste. My preference is to use sea salt; because of its fuller flavor, less is needed as compared to ordinary table salt. Be sure to taste before adding salt, since it is an ingredient in canned chicken broth, tomatoes, and beans (unless you specifically select unsalted products).

- Cooking times are always approximate and may vary somewhat by pan type and weight, the use of a gas or electric stove, differences in microwaves, and, in some cases, the thickness of the chicken. It is important to judge by appearances (which are described), such as chicken that is lightly browned and cooked through (meaning no longer pink in the center of the thickest points), vegetables that are crisp-tender, or pasta that is *al dente* (firm to the bite). As you become familiar with my recipes, you will easily be able to judge the cooking time by the way the food looks, smells, or tastes.

- All of the recipes, including the soups and salads, make entrées of generous proportions. In smaller portions, some could serve as starters or side dishes. For serving larger groups, all of the recipes can easily be doubled. In these instances, chopping, bringing liquids to a boil, and cooking may increase the preparation time a bit over 15 minutes. When doubling recipes, use $1^1/_2$ times the amount of herbs and spices called for; taste and adjust the amounts.

- Advance preparation tips have been included whenever applicable. Often, a dressing or sauce can be made ahead of time, then paired with freshly cooked chicken and vegetables. Some recipes, such as the soups, can be refrigerated for reheating and serving later. Consider the advance preparation information as a guide for using leftovers, too.

- When reheating recipes prepared ahead, take care not to overcook the chicken or vegetables. Be especially cautious if using a microwave; stovetop heating allows you to keep an eye on the pan.

- For entertaining, I always cut up the chicken and vegetables in advance; I also organize other ingredients, accompaniments, equipment, and serving plates. Whenever possible, I mix sauces or dressings. This eliminates last-minute mess and reduces my time in the kitchen.

- Variations are suggestions for alternate cooking methods or ingredients; these suggestions encourage you to use ingredients you have on hand, your favorite flavors, or in-season produce. Allow my recipes to serve as an inspiration for your own ideas and variations. If you are a novice in the kitchen, I assure you this will come naturally after you become familiar with the procedures and gain confidence. (Keep in mind that variations, such as adding ingredients, may increase preparation time; and additions and changes will alter the nutrition values.)

- Suggestions for garnishes are included with most recipes. They are optional, but select one, two, or a few. Be creative; let the artist in you emerge.

- Explanations of many items, especially the ethnic and less-common ingredients, and certain techniques are provided in the Tips. Refer to page references in the index.

- Each of the recipes includes a nutritional analysis per serving, based on the stated number of servings that the recipe yields. The ingredients have been analyzed in the form as listed, such as "low-fat yogurt," "reduced-fat cholesterol-free mayonnaise," or "low-sodium soy sauce." Dressings and sauces are included, as are the amounts of marinade that are absorbed. Garnishes and variations will alter the figures; suggested accompaniments such as pasta or rice are not included unless they are ingredients incorporated into the recipes. Use the analyses to help you meet your daily dietary goals.

Cooking Efficiently

One of the best kitchen time-savers is one of the oldest principles of French cooking—*mise en place*. It means "everything in place"—ingredients prepared and equipment assembled before cooking begins. For the 15-minute practitioner, this means setting out the necessary pans and utensils and preheating the oven or broiler, if necessary. Organize all of the items in the ingredient list. Clean the vegetables and fruits to prepare for chopping. Because the recipes are quick to prepare, as your first step it may be necessary to attend to the accompaniments, such as heating precooked rice, preparing basmati rice (which requires only 15 minutes), or bringing water to a boil for cooking pasta. Then let the clock begin. Follow the sequence of steps as described, and in just 15 minutes—and that includes chopping time—your dinner will be on the table.

The most important thing to remember is that efficient cooking does not follow a linear progression. As you proceed, it is not necessary to complete one step before going on to another. Instead, without a lot of fuss, you can actually do two things at once, such as mixing a sauce or dressing or chopping vegetables while your chicken cooks on the grill. By following the plan outlined in the recipes, you can have your entire meal ready to eat at the same time. Although some of the ingredient lists may appear long, they still adhere to our 15-minute timetable, for the number of ingredients requiring chopping has been kept to a minimum. Chopping efficiency is enhanced with a good, sharp set of knives; your food processor can be used for preparations like grating carrots or chopping onions.

And now, begin. This streamlined approach to preparing gourmet chicken dishes enables me to cook outstanding meals every night of the week. When I entertain, I do it with casual elegance, using 15-minute recipes that allow me time to enjoy my guests. Why spend hours in the kitchen when you can produce delicious chicken entrées in just 15 minutes? These recipes can free you, too, from tedious kitchen duties while adding style and good nutrition to your meals.

When your creation is ready to serve, present it with style. As I tell my cooking students, you can be a quick, efficient cook, but no one needs to know you spent only 15 minutes preparing dinner. Serve your creations on attractive plates. Then garnish! Even the simplest of garnishes, like a sprig of fresh herb, can make your meal seem to be the work of a trained chef rather than a hurried cook. Quite simply, you will create the impression that you prepared the meal with care. And I guarantee it will be delicious!

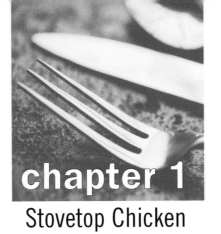

chapter 1
Stovetop Chicken

SKINLESS, BONELESS CHICKEN BREAST HALVES ARE

a natural for stovetop cooking. And recipes using the stove-

top methods of sautéing, stir-frying, and braising require

minimal equipment and can easily be completed in 15

minutes. Since most of these recipes incorporate vegeta-

bles along with the chicken, these are one-dish meals,

requiring the simple addition of pasta, couscous, or bas-

mati rice. In some, the rice or pasta is incorporated into

the recipe.

Sautéing, also called pan-frying, requires only a fraction of the fat necessary for frying. The name comes from the French verb *sauter*, which means "to jump"; here the chicken is kept in motion by stirring or tossing. For proper sautéing, you will need a good, heavy skillet. I prefer one that is 10 or 12 inches in diameter so the chicken will not be crowded. I use a pan with a nonstick surface and, if necessary, a tight-fitting lid. To prepare the chicken for sautéing, rinse the chicken breasts and pat dry with a paper towel. It is important to remove any surface moisture because it will inhibit browning.

Using just enough oil to prevent the chicken from sticking (quantities are based upon the use of a nonstick pan), heat the oil over medium-high heat before the chicken is added. If you prefer, with a nonstick pan you can sauté using nonstick cooking spray or a small amount of chicken broth. (Your stove and pan will determine the heat setting. If the cooking surface is too hot, the exterior of the chicken may become dark and crispy while the interior remains raw. If it's too low, the chicken may overcook and toughen.) Cook the chicken until it is golden brown on all sides and the centers at the thickest points are no longer pink. Since the chicken breasts in these recipes are cut into small pieces or strips, this will take about 5 minutes. Use tongs for turning the chicken as it cooks; a fork or sharp instrument will pierce the flesh and allow the juices to escape. Cooked properly, the inside of the chicken will remain juicy and tender.

Stir-frying over high or medium-high heat (depending upon the stove and the pan) cooks the food quickly as it is constantly and briskly stirred and tossed with a spatula or large spoon. Woks are the traditional pan used for this method; however, they are not necessarily the best choice for stovetop cooking. Horizontal pans with wide bottoms are a better choice. I use a nonstick 12-inch skillet or sauté pan so that the food is never more than an inch deep.

Since stir-fries go well with rice, I often cook rice in advance and reheat it as the chicken and vegetables cook. For last-minute preparation, I choose a quick-to-prepare accompaniment such as basmati rice, Chinese wheat-flour noodles, or couscous.

The key to successful stir-frying is preparing all of the ingredients before you begin cooking. Pat the ingredients dry to prevent spattering as the food cooks. The chicken should be cut into bite-size pieces (see page xviii for tips on cutting partially frozen chicken). Many supermarkets sell precut "chicken for stir-frying"; check the labels to be certain no flavorings have been added. Each type of vegetable, whether sliced or cut into small cubes or strips, should be cut into uniform pieces so they will cook evenly. Most produce departments have precut "vegetables for stir-frying"; this is a time-saver, but be aware that cutting vegetables closer to cooking time will minimize nutrient loss.

When you are ready to cook, begin by combining your sauce ingredients. Set the sauce aside and heat the pan; it is hot enough when water droplets make a sizzling sound and bounce. Heat the oil and cook the chicken first, stir-frying until it is just cooked through. Using a slotted spoon to keep the juices and oil in the pan, remove the chicken, cover it, and set aside. Additional oil may need to be heated before adding the vegetables. Begin by cooking the firmest ingredients (carrots, broccoli, cauliflower); onions also need to be added early to allow the flavor to develop. The softest vegetables are added last (zucchini, snow peas, mushrooms, tomatoes, and fresh, tender greens); herbs and aromatic ingredients such as garlic, ginger, and chives should also be added toward the end of cooking. Last, reduce the heat, transfer the chicken back to the pan, and stir in the sauce to coat all ingredients and thicken the liquid. Serve the stir-fry mixture at once; if the pan is covered to keep the contents warm, the vegetables will lose their crispness.

For entertaining, I chop all of the ingredients in advance, dividing them into three or four separate bowls (sauce, chicken, firm vegetables, and soft vegetables). I cook a pot of rice in my rice cooker and hold it on the "warm" setting. The stir-fry must be cooked just before serving. If the ingredients are well organized, from the time I begin cooking, dinner can be on the table in 10 minutes.

Stir-fries offer innumerable exciting possibilities for variations. It is not necessary to stick to typically Asian vegetables; nearly any vegetable can be used. As you vary the recipes, remember that the quantity of sauce in my recipes will accommodate 12 ounces of chicken and 4 to 5 cups of vegetables.

Braising is a cooking method in which the chicken is first sautéed until brown but not totally cooked; it is then simmered in a liquid that contains vegetables, herbs, and spices. During this moist-cooking stage, the flavor of the chicken combines with the other ingredients, resulting in tender, tasty meat and a rich-tasting sauce. To make the most of the juices from the chicken and to accommodate the added liquid, a nonstick 10- or 12-inch sauté pan (one with straight sides) is the best choice. A tight-fitting lid is important to keep the liquid from evaporating as the dish cooks.

The sauce for many braised dishes is thickened with cornstarch. To prevent lumping, the cornstarch should be dissolved in cold water before combining with the other sauce ingredients. The result is a fairly clear liquid rather than a sauce with the cloudy appearance caused by flour thickening.

For 15-minute efficiency, the first step is to chop the vegetables and set out the other ingredients; in some recipes the sauce ingredients are stirred together before beginning to cook. After rinsing and cutting the chicken into strips to ensure quick cooking, the pieces should be patted dry. Both sides of the strips are then lightly pressed into a seasoned flour mixture; be sure to shake off excess flour. (If you prefer, the chicken strips can be tossed with the flour mixture in a sealed plastic bag; this is quicker but does not coat the chicken quite as evenly.) As they are prepared, place the strips on a plate so that you can add them all at the same time to the heated oil in the sauté pan.

After cooking just 2 minutes per side over medium-high heat, the chicken strips will be lightly browned but not cooked through. After the sauce is stirred in, cover the pan while the entire mixture cooks for about 8 minutes—long enough for the chicken to be cooked through and the vegetables to become tender.

bell pepper–
rosemary
chicken

Makes 4 servings

The colorful array of bell peppers now available in our supermarkets inspired this recipe. Don't hesitate to substitute others, such as purple or orange bell peppers; all bell peppers are mild with only subtle variations in flavor. Serve this over egg noodles or rice.

2 tablespoons olive oil, divided

12 ounces boneless skinless chicken breast halves, cut into 2-inch-long by $3/8$-inch-wide strips

1 red bell pepper, cut into 3-inch-long by $3/8$-inch-wide strips

1 yellow bell pepper, cut into 3-inch-long by $3/8$-inch-wide strips

$1/2$ green bell pepper, cut into 3-inch-long by $3/8$-inch-wide strips

1 medium onion, cut into 3-inch-long by $1/4$-inch-wide strips (about 1 cup)

$1/4$ cup fresh lemon juice

2 teaspoons minced fresh rosemary (or $1/2$ teaspoon dried rosemary, crushed); (see Tip)

$1/2$ teaspoon pepper, or to taste

GARNISH (OPTIONAL) freshly ground black pepper, freshly grated Parmesan cheese, toasted pine nuts

1. Heat 1 tablespoon of the oil in a large nonstick skillet or sauté pan over medium-high heat. Add the chicken; cook, stirring occasionally, for about 5 minutes or until it is lightly browned and cooked through.

(continues)

2. With a slotted spoon, transfer the chicken to a bowl and cover to keep warm.

3. Heat the remaining 1 tablespoon of oil in the skillet. Add the bell peppers and onion; cook, stirring occasionally, for about 5 minutes or until tender. Reduce the heat to medium; add the cooked chicken, lemon juice, rosemary, and pepper; stir gently for about 1 minute or until heated through. Adjust the seasoning to taste.

4. To serve, spoon the pepper-chicken mixture over beds of pasta or rice.

PER SERVING: Cal 210/Prot 25.3g/Carb 6g/Fat 9.4g/Chol 65mg/Sod 55mg

ADVANCE PREPARATION   The chicken-pepper mixture can be made 1 day in advance: Slightly undercook the peppers. Reheat and serve over freshly cooked, hot noodles or rice.

TIP

To enhance the flavor and reduce the splintery texture of dried rosemary, crush the leaves between your fingers just before adding to the recipe. Rosemary has a bold taste, especially in dried form; use it sparingly.

Bell Pepper–Rosemary Chicken

paprika chicken

Makes 4 servings

Supermarket paprika will do in a pinch, but this recipe really shines when you use imported Hungarian paprika, found in specialty stores and gourmet shops. This updated version of the traditional Hungarian classic uses yogurt in place of sour cream. Serve atop egg noodles or rice.

3/4 cup chicken broth

2 tablespoons tomato paste

2 teaspoons sweet Hungarian paprika, or to taste (see Tip)

1 tablespoon minced fresh thyme (or 1/2 teaspoon dried thyme)

1/2 teaspoon pepper

1/3 cup low-fat plain yogurt

2 teaspoons all-purpose flour

1 tablespoon olive oil

3 cups sliced mushrooms

1/2 cup finely chopped onion

2 teaspoons minced garlic

1 pound boneless skinless chicken breast halves, cut into 1-inch pieces

GARNISH (OPTIONAL) dash of paprika and minced flat-leaf parsley

1. Stir together the chicken broth, tomato paste, paprika, thyme, and pepper in a measuring cup. Set aside.

2. In a separate measuring cup or small bowl, stir together the yogurt and flour. Set aside.

3. Heat the oil in a large nonstick sauté pan over medium-high heat. Add the mushrooms, onion, and garlic; cook, stirring occasionally, for about 5 minutes or until the vegetables are softened but not browned.

4. Add the chicken to the pan, stirring for about 2 minutes or until it is no longer pink on the outside. Stir in the chicken broth mixture.

5. Reduce the heat to medium; cover and cook for about 5 minutes or until the sauce is bubbly and the chicken is cooked through.

6. Reduce the heat to low; add the yogurt mixture, stirring constantly until slightly thickened. (Do not allow the mixture to come to a boil.)

7. To assemble the servings, spoon a bed of noodles or rice onto four plates. Top each with the chicken mixture.

PER SERVING: Cal 254/Prot 36.7g/Carb 9.2g/Fat 7.8g/Chol 88mg/Sod 264mg

> ## TIP
>
> Paprika is a powder made from ground aromatic sweet red pepper pods. The flavor can range from mild to pungent and hot, and the color from red-orange to deep red. Most paprika comes from Spain, South America, California, or Hungary; the Hungarian variety is considered by many to be the best. Hungarian paprika comes in three levels of hotness: mild (also called "sweet"), hot, and exceptionally hot. To preserve its color and flavor, paprika should be stored in a cool, dark place for no longer than 6 months.

chicken fajitas

Makes 4 servings (3 tortillas each)

Fajitas, a dish from south of the border, have become very popular in restaurants here, where they are served in many variations. This simple version is a meal in itself.

$1/4$ cup fresh lime juice

2 teaspoons chili powder

1 teaspoon minced garlic

$1/2$ teaspoon pepper, or to taste

$1/4$ teaspoon ground cumin

1 pound boneless skinless chicken breast halves, cut into 2-inch-long by $1/4$-inch-wide strips

1 tablespoon olive oil

1 red bell pepper, cut into 2-inch-long by $1/4$-inch-wide strips

1 green bell pepper, cut into 2-inch-long by $1/4$-inch-wide strips

1 medium onion, sliced (about 1 cup)

1 tablespoon minced jalapeño pepper, or to taste

12 (6- or 7-inch) flour tortillas (white or whole wheat); (see Tip)

1. Combine the lime juice, chili powder, garlic, pepper, and ground cumin in a medium bowl. Add the chicken strips and toss; set aside for 5 to 10 minutes, stirring occasionally.

2. Heat the oil in a large nonstick sauté pan over medium-high heat. Add the bell peppers, onion, and jalapeño pepper; cook, stirring occasionally, for about 4 minutes or until the peppers are crisp-tender. Add the chicken mixture, with lime juice marinade; cook, stirring occasionally, for about 5 minutes or until the chicken is cooked through and the vegetables are softened. Adjust the seasonings to taste.

3. Place the tortillas between two paper towels. Microwave on high for about 15 to 20 seconds or until they are moist and warm. (Or wrap the tortillas in aluminum foil and heat in a 350°F oven for about 10 minutes.)

4. To serve, place the warm tortillas on a plate; cover to keep warm. Spoon the chicken-vegetable mixture into a bowl. Assemble the fajitas as you eat by spooning some of the chicken mixture into the center third of each tortilla and rolling the sides.

PER SERVING: Cal 523/Prot 41.6g/Carb 60.6g/Fat 12.7g/Chol 87mg/Sod 149mg

ADVANCE PREPARATION   This dish tastes best when served immediately; but, if necessary, the chicken mixture can be prepared several hours before serving, then refrigerated, and reheated just prior to serving.

> **TIP**
>
> Tortillas are found on Mexican tables at nearly every meal. In the corn-producing regions of the South, tortillas are usually made from corn; however, in the northern areas, where wheat is grown, flour tortillas are favored. Corn and flour tortillas, both white and whole wheat, are found in most supermarkets, refrigerated or frozen.

Variations

- Substitute other vegetables for the bell peppers (up to 2 cups total). Try strips of zucchini or summer squash, or oil-packed sun-dried tomatoes, drained and coarsely chopped.

- Add about 1/4 cup coarsely chopped fresh cilantro to the chicken-vegetable mixture.

- When rolling the tortillas, in addition to the chicken mixture, add coarsely chopped tomatoes, shredded lettuce, plain yogurt, nonfat sour cream, and/or shredded cheese (Cheddar or Monterey Jack).

- For a nontraditional version, spread a layer of chèvre cheese or crumbled feta cheese on the tortilla before adding the chicken and vegetables.

chicken
with **curried**
peaches

Makes 4 servings

Curry makes a flavor statement here; it's a natural mate to chicken and fruit. Because there is a wide variation in the intensity of curry powders, adjust the amount to suit your taste. I like to serve this with basmati rice, steamed vegetables, a green salad, and crusty bread.

1 tablespoon olive oil

$^1/_4$ cup water

1 tablespoon curry powder, or to taste

1 pound boneless skinless chicken breast halves, cut into 1-inch pieces

$^1/_2$ cup fresh orange juice

1 tablespoon light brown sugar

1 teaspoon finely minced fresh ginger

4 peaches (at room temperature), peeled, pitted, and cut into $^1/_4$-inch wedges (see Tips)

GARNISH (OPTIONAL)   toasted coarsely chopped walnuts

1. Heat the oil in a large nonstick sauté pan over medium-high heat. Add the water, stir in the curry powder, and heat until bubbly.

2. Add the chicken and cook, covered, stirring occasionally for about 5 minutes or until it is lightly browned and cooked through.

3. With a slotted spoon, transfer the chicken to a bowl and cover to keep warm.

4. Meanwhile, combine the orange juice, brown sugar, and ginger in a measuring cup; stir until the sugar is dissolved.

5. Add the peaches and orange juice mixture to the sauté pan; stir for about 3 minutes or until the fruit is lightly cooked and the sauce is bubbly. Add the chicken; stir gently for about 1 minute or until the mixture is warmed through. Adjust the seasoning to taste.

6. Spoon the chicken mixture over beds of rice on individual serving plates.

PER SERVING: Cal 269/Prot 33.9g/Carb 17.1g/Fat 7.2g/Chol 87mg/Sod 73mg

Variations

- Substitute fresh pears for the peaches.

- Substitute 3 cups frozen peach wedges for the fresh peaches; thaw in advance and follow the same procedure, taking care not to over-cook the fruit.

- Substitute other fruits for the peaches. Try one (10-ounce) can "lite" sliced peaches, pear slices, pineapple chunks, apricots, or a mixture. Drain, reserving 1/2 cup juice, which may be used in place of the orange juice. Omit the brown sugar and cook only until the sauce is bubbly and the fruit is warm.

TIPS

- Choose peaches that are firm to slightly soft with a yellow or creamy skin color. To speed up ripening, place peaches in a paper bag with an apple and let stand at room temperature for 2 to 3 days. When fully ripe, keep them in a sealed bag in the refrigerator; use within a few days.

- To peel a peach, immerse it in boiling water for 1 minute. Then drop the peach into cold water. Remove the peel with firm downward pulls.

chicken and morels
with honey-mustard
sauce

Makes 4 servings

Fresh morels are generally available in April; depending upon growing conditions, the season may last into June. For the ideal menu to welcome spring, mound this aromatic mixture on egg noodles or rice and drizzle some of the sauce over steamed slender fresh asparagus on the side.

Honey-Mustard Sauce

1/4 cup Dijon mustard

3 tablespoons honey

2 tablespoons minced fresh tarragon (or
   1/2 teaspoon dried tarragon)

1/4 teaspoon pepper

1/2 cup half-and-half

Dash of salt

To Complete the Recipe

1 tablespoon olive oil

12 ounces boneless skinless chicken
   breast halves, cut into 2-inch-long by
   1/2-inch-wide strips

4 ounces fresh morel mushrooms, halved
   if very large (about 1 1/2 cups or
   16 mushrooms); (see Tip)

2 tablespoons minced shallot

GARNISH (OPTIONAL) freshly ground black pepper, sprigs of fresh tarragon, basil, or flat-leaf parsley

1. To prepare the sauce, combine the mustard and honey in a small bowl or measuring cup. Stir in the remaining ingredients; set aside.

2. To prepare the chicken and morels, heat the oil in a large nonstick sauté pan over medium-high heat. Add the chicken strips and cook, stirring occasionally, for about 3 minutes or until they are lightly browned but not cooked through. Add the mushrooms and shallot. Continue cooking, stirring constantly, for about 3 minutes or until the mushrooms are tender and the chicken is cooked through.

3. Reduce the heat to low. Stir the sauce and pour it over the chicken and mushrooms. Stir gently until the sauce is warm and evenly distributed.

4. Serve over egg noodles or rice.

PER SERVING: Cal 257/Prot 26.3g/Carb 16.4g/Fat 9.6g/Chol 76mg/Sod 109mg

Variations

- Substitute fresh or dried basil for the tarragon.

- Substitute milk for the half-and-half.

- Substitute other mushrooms, such as cremini, for the morels.

- Substitute 1 ounce dried morels for 4 ounces fresh. Before adding to the recipe, soak the dried morels in 1 cup of warm water for about 30 minutes (for added flavor, soak the mushrooms in warm sherry, brandy, or broth); or boil for about 2 to 5 minutes. As the water is absorbed, turn the mushrooms occasionally and add more water if necessary. For maximum flavor, use only as much water as the mushrooms will absorb. Drain well before adding to the recipe.

> **TIP**
>
> Morels are edible wild mushrooms belonging to the truffle family. The flavor is smoky, earthy, and nutty; in general, the darker the mushroom, the stronger the flavor. Choose fresh mushrooms with a firm yet spongy texture. Refrigerate them in a single layer covered with a damp towel; avoid airtight plastic bags. Do not eat raw morels; they must be cooked. Dried morels, available year-round, have a more intense flavor than fresh; they can be substituted in recipes after being rehydrated (see Variations). To remove traces of sand, both fresh and dried morels should be well rinsed before using.

sweet-and-sour chicken

Makes 4 servings

Unlike the popular restaurant versions made with deep-fried chicken, this Sweet-and-Sour Chicken begins with just a quick stir-fry. A typical Chinese sweet-sour sauce, made with a mixture of sugar and vinegar with soy sauce, is a flavor combination that balances the sweet and tart elements so that one does not overpower the other, yet both can be detected and savored.

Sweet-and-Sour Sauce

1 tablespoon cold water

1 tablespoon cornstarch (see Tips)

1 cup apple juice

1/4 cup white rice vinegar

2 tablespoons tomato paste

1 tablespoon low-sodium soy sauce

1 tablespoon honey

1 tablespoon finely minced fresh ginger

1/4 teaspoon ground white pepper

To Complete the Recipe

3 teaspoons canola or safflower oil, divided

12 ounces boneless skinless chicken
  breast halves, cut into 2-inch-long by
  1/2-inch-wide strips

1 red bell pepper, cut into 2-inch-long by
  1/4-inch-wide strips

1 carrot, cut into 1/8-inch-thick slices

1 small onion, sliced (about 1/2 cup)

1 teaspoon minced garlic

1 (8-ounce) can unsweetened pineapple
chunks, drained

GARNISH (OPTIONAL)   toasted sesame seeds, sprigs of fresh cilantro, scallion curls (see Tips)

1. To prepare the sauce, stir together the water and cornstarch in a small bowl or 2-cup measure until smooth. Stir in the remaining ingredients; set aside.

2. To prepare the chicken, heat 2 teaspoons of the oil in a large nonstick sauté pan or wok over medium-high heat. Add the chicken; stir-fry for about 5 minutes or until it is lightly browned and cooked through.

3. With a slotted spoon, transfer the chicken to a bowl and cover to keep warm.

4. Add the remaining 1 teaspoon of oil to the sauté pan. Stir-fry the bell pepper, carrot, and onion for about 3 minutes or until the carrot is crisp-tender. Add the garlic; continue to stir-fry for about 30 seconds.

5. Reduce the heat to low. Stir the sauce; pour it over the vegetables and stir constantly for about 30 seconds or until the sauce thickens slightly. Add the chicken and pineapple chunks; stir gently until heated through.

6. Spoon the Sweet-and-Sour Chicken over beds of rice or Chinese wheat-flour noodles.

PER SERVING: Cal 264/Prot 26.2g/Carb 25.7g/Fat 6.3g/Chol 65mg/Sod 208mg

Variations

*   Substitute other vegetables for the bell pepper and carrot (up to 2 cups total). Try broccoli, asparagus, or sliced mushrooms.

*   Stir in 2 plum tomatoes cut into wedges when you add the pineapple chunks.

TIPS

*   Cornstarch, a fine white flour obtained from corn, is used as a thickener. It gives sauces, puddings, gravies, etc., a glossy, almost transparent look, as opposed to the cloudy appearance provided by flour thickening. Cornstarch works best when mixed with enough cold water to form a smooth, thin paste, then added to a hot mixture near the end of cooking time. Stir constantly but gently as you add the cornstarch mixture, and cook just long enough to thicken. Mixtures thickened with cornstarch tend to thin if cooked too long, at a high temperature, or if not stirred gently.

*   To make scallion curls, slice the green part of the scallion very thinly lengthwise. Drop into a bowl of ice water; curls will form in about 10 to 15 minutes.

chicken
and **vegetable**
curry

Makes 4 servings

My favorite accompaniment for this recipe is basmati rice. For variety, I sometimes add a peeled and coarsely chopped apple along with the tomato.

1 cup broccoli florets

2 carrots, cut into thin diagonal slices

1 small onion, cut into 1/4-inch-thick wedges (about 1/2 cup)

1 tablespoon canola or safflower oil

12 ounces boneless skinless chicken breasts, cut into 2-inch-long by 1/2-inch-wide strips

Curry Sauce

1 tablespoon canola or safflower oil

1 tablespoon curry powder, or to taste

2 tablespoons finely minced fresh ginger

2 teaspoons minced jalapeño pepper (or 1/4 teaspoon red pepper flakes), or to taste

1 teaspoon minced garlic

1 cup water

1 tablespoon fresh lime juice

To Complete the Recipe

1 cup frozen peas (preferably baby peas), thawed

2 plum tomatoes, each cut into 8 wedges

GARNISH (OPTIONAL)   dry-roasted unsalted peanuts or toasted sesame seeds, sprigs of fresh cilantro

1. To prepare the vegetables and chicken, put the broccoli, carrots, and onion in a medium microwave-proof dish; add about $1/4$ cup water. Cover and microwave on high for about 6 minutes or until the vegetables are tender. Drain well; cover to keep warm. (Or cook the vegetables for about 6 to 8 minutes in a stovetop steamer.)

2. Meanwhile, heat the oil in a medium nonstick skillet over medium-high heat. Add the chicken; cook, stirring occasionally, for about 5 minutes or until it is lightly browned and cooked through.

3. While the vegetables and chicken are cooking, prepare the sauce: Heat the oil in a large sauté pan over medium heat. Add the curry powder, ginger, jalapeño pepper (if using), and garlic; stir for 1 minute. Add the water and bring the mixture to a boil; cook, uncovered, for about 3 minutes or until the sauce is reduced slightly. Remove from the heat; stir in the lime juice and red pepper flakes (if using).

4. Stir the broccoli, carrots, onion, and chicken strips into the sauce. Add the peas and tomato wedges; toss gently until warmed through. Adjust the seasonings to taste.

5. Spoon rice into four shallow bowls; top with the chicken and vegetable curry.

PER SERVING: Cal 274/Prot 28.8g/Carb 16.7g/Fat 10.2g/Chol 65mg/Sod 133mg

ADVANCE PREPARATION   This dish is best when served immediately. For do-ahead preparation, cook up to 1 day in advance, but omit the tomatoes until you reheat the mixture just prior to serving. Keep in mind that the flavor of curry often intensifies when the dish is allowed to sit.

Variation

- Substitute other vegetables for the broccoli and carrots (up to 3 cups total). Try cauliflower florets, chunks of new potatoes, or sautéed sliced mushrooms.

walnut chicken
with sherry sauce

Makes 4 servings

Because both sherry and soy sauce are salty, use unsalted chicken broth in this recipe. Vary the vegetables and, for another intriguing flavor combination, try substituting sesame seeds and dark sesame oil for the walnuts and walnut oil.

Sherry Sauce

1 tablespoon cold water

2 teaspoons cornstarch

3/4 cup unsalted chicken broth

1/4 cup low-sodium soy sauce

2 tablespoons dry sherry

1 teaspoon finely minced fresh ginger

1 teaspoon minced garlic

Dash of ground white pepper

To Complete the Recipe

3 teaspoons canola or safflower oil, divided

1 pound boneless skinless chicken breast halves, cut into 2-inch-long by 1/2-inch-wide strips

3 cups green beans in 2-inch pieces

3 medium scallions, cut into 2-inch lengths

1/4 cup coarsely chopped walnuts (see Tips)

1 teaspoon walnut oil (preferably toasted walnut oil)

GARNISH (OPTIONAL)   sprigs of fresh flat-leaf parsley (see Tips)

1. To prepare the sauce, stir together the water and cornstarch in a small bowl or 2-cup measure until smooth. Stir in the remaining sauce ingredients; set aside.

2. To prepare the chicken, heat 2 teaspoons of the canola or safflower oil in a large non-stick sauté pan or wok over medium-high heat. Add the chicken and stir-fry for about 5 minutes or until it is lightly browned and cooked through.

3. With a slotted spoon, transfer the chicken to a bowl and cover to keep warm.

4. Heat the remaining 1 teaspoon of canola or safflower oil in the same pan. Add the green beans; stir-fry for about 5 minutes. Add the scallions; continue to stir-fry for about 2 minutes or until the beans are crisp-tender.

5. Reduce the heat to medium. Stir the sauce and pour it over the vegetables, stirring gently for about 30 seconds or until it is thickened and clear. Reduce the heat to low; stir in the chicken, walnuts, and walnut oil.

6. To serve, spoon rice onto individual serving plates; top with the stir-fry mixture.

PER SERVING: Cal 370/Prot 40.6g/Carb 13.3g/Fat 17.1g/Chol 87mg/Sod 707mg

Variations

- Substitute other vegetables for the green beans (up to 3 cups total). Try broccoli florets, cut asparagus, red bell pepper strips, or stemmed snow peas.

- Substitute dark sesame oil for the walnut oil and $1/4$ cup toasted sesame seeds for the walnuts.

> **TIPS**
>
> - Black walnuts are stronger in flavor than English (or Persian) walnuts. Use either kind in this recipe.
>
> - Flat-leaf, or Italian, parsley has a more pungent flavor than the more common curly-leaf parsley. Wash fresh parsley, shake off the excess moisture, and wrap first in paper towels, then in a plastic bag. Refrigerate for up to 1 week. Avoid dried parsley, which has little of the distinctive parsley flavor.

chapter 1 *Stovetop Chicken*

Korean

KoreanKorean

Korean

Korean

Korean

chicken
with **chinese**
tahini sauce

Makes 4 servings

The combination of flavors in this Szechuan-type sauce is both fiery and absolutely wonderful! But feel free to adjust the amount of chili paste with garlic to suit your taste. This is particularly tasty when served over a bed of Chinese wheat-flour noodles—or you can use buckwheat (soba) noodles, couscous, bulgur wheat, or rice.

Chinese Tahini Sauce

1/4 cup tahini (see Tips)

1 tablespoon chili paste with garlic, or to taste (see Tips)

1/2 cup water, or as needed

To Complete the Recipe

4 cups broccoli florets

1 carrot, halved lengthwise and cut into 1/8-inch-thick slices

1 tablespoon canola or safflower oil

12 ounces boneless skinless chicken breast halves, cut into 1-inch pieces

GARNISH (OPTIONAL)   toasted sesame seeds, sprigs of fresh cilantro

1. To prepare the sauce, combine the tahini and chili paste with garlic in a small bowl. Add the water and stir until smooth. (The sauce should have a cake-batter consistency; add water as needed.) Set aside.

2. To prepare the vegetables, put the broccoli and carrot in a large microwave-proof dish; add about 1/4 cup water. Cover and cook in the microwave on high for about 6 minutes

or until they are crisp-tender (see Tips). Drain well; cover to keep warm. (Or cook the broccoli and carrots for about 6 to 8 minutes in a stovetop steamer.)

3. Meanwhile, heat the oil in a large nonstick sauté pan over medium-high heat. Add the chicken; stir-fry for about 5 minutes or until it is lightly browned and cooked through.

4. Reduce the heat to low. Add the broccoli, carrot, and sauce; stir gently until the sauce and chicken are heated through. Adjust the seasoning to taste.

5. Spoon over individual servings of noodles, couscous, or rice.

PER SERVING: Cal 328/Prot 32g/Carb 9.9g/Fat 17.8g/Chol 65mg/Sod 134mg

Variation

• Substitute other vegetables for the broccoli and carrot (up to 5 cups total). Try asparagus or green beans.

TIPS

• Tahini, a paste made by grinding sesame seeds, is also called sesame butter. The darker variety, made from toasted sesame seeds, is stronger in flavor than the lighter variety. Stir before using to reincorporate oil. Keep tahini refrigerated, but bring to room temperature before using.

• Chili paste with garlic—sometimes labeled Chinese chili paste, chili purée with garlic, or Chinese chili sauce—is available in the ethnic-foods aisle of most supermarkets. A hot, spicy sauce made from chilies, rice vinegar, garlic, and salt, it is used in Szechuan cooking and as a condiment. Store the tightly closed container in the refrigerator.

• Microwave cooking time depends on the wattage and size of your microwave oven. It is also affected by the freshness, moisture content, maturity, and quantity of vegetables you're cooking. To hold in the steam, cover the cooking container with a lid or heavy-duty plastic wrap. Test for doneness at the minimum suggested cooking time; if necessary, microwave further in 1-minute increments. Food continues to cook after it is removed from the microwave, so remove it 1 minute or so before it would be done.

asian
chicken strips
with **lemon-sesame**
sauce

Makes 4 servings

This lemon-sesame sauce boasts a citrus flavor with a hint of sesame oil—an interesting complement to crispy chicken strips. Serve this dish with rice, couscous, or Chinese wheat-flour noodles. Steamed vegetables, such as asparagus or broccoli florets, are a nice addition; but, when available, I like to top off the feast with portobello mushrooms sautéed with fresh ginger and garlic.

Lemon-Sesame Sauce

$1/4$ cup low-sodium soy sauce (see Tip)

1 teaspoon lemon zest

$1/4$ cup fresh lemon juice

1 tablespoon dark sesame oil

1 teaspoon minced garlic

1 teaspoon sugar

To Complete the Recipe

$1/4$ cup all-purpose flour

1 teaspoon sesame seeds

$1/2$ teaspoon pepper

1 tablespoon canola or safflower oil

1 pound boneless skinless chicken breast
   halves, cut into 2-inch-long by
   $1/2$-inch-wide strips

4 large leaves curly leaf lettuce

1 (15-ounce) can mandarin orange
segments, drained

1. To prepare the sauce, combine the ingredients in a small bowl or measuring cup, stirring to dissolve the sugar. Set aside.

2. To prepare the chicken, spoon the flour, sesame seeds, and pepper into a plastic bag. Add the chicken strips, close the bag tightly, and shake to coat the chicken.

3. Heat the oil in a large nonstick skillet over medium-high heat. Add the chicken strips in a single layer; cook for about 3 minutes or until they are crisp and golden on the bottom. Turn the chicken; continue to cook for about 2 minutes or until the strips are cooked through.

4. While the chicken is cooking, line serving plates with the leaf lettuce. Place the warm, cooked chicken on the greens. Surround with mandarin orange segments. Stir the sauce and drizzle about 2 tablespoons over each serving. Serve the remaining sauce in a container on the side.

PER SERVING: Cal 277/Prot 35.4g/Carb 11.7g/Fat 9.8g/Chol 87mg/Sod 628mg

ADVANCE PREPARATION   The lemon-sesame sauce can be made up to a day in advance and refrigerated; bring to room temperature before serving with the warm chicken strips.

> **TIP**
>
> Low-sodium or "lite" soy sauce contains about 40 percent less sodium than traditional soy sauce or tamari, but it provides nearly the same flavor. Soy sauce will keep almost indefinitely if refrigerated.

mediterranean
chicken
with penne

Makes 4 servings

This dish was born of happy memories of al fresco feasts I have enjoyed during my travels throughout southern Europe. I usually serve this dish warm as a hearty dinner; but the left-overs, served chilled or at room temperature, become a deluxe lunch the next day.

Dash of salt

8 ounces penne (about 3 cups)

2 tablespoons olive oil, divided

8 ounces boneless skinless chicken breast halves, cut into 1-inch pieces

1 small eggplant, peeled and cut into $^{1}/_{2}$-inch cubes (about 2 cups); (see Tips)

4 plum tomatoes, cut into $^{1}/_{2}$-inch cubes (about 2 cups)

1 cup sliced mushrooms

$^{1}/_{4}$ cup minced shallots

2 tablespoons minced fresh thyme (or 1 teaspoon dried thyme); (see Tips)

$^{1}/_{2}$ teaspoon pepper, or to taste

$^{1}/_{4}$ cup red wine vinegar

2 tablespoons capers, drained and rinsed

GARNISH (OPTIONAL) freshly ground black pepper, crumbled feta cheese, sprigs of fresh thyme

1. Bring a large pot of water to a boil over high heat; add salt, then the penne. When the water returns to a boil, stir occasionally to separate the penne. Reduce the heat to medium-high and cook for about 10 to 12 minutes, or according to package instructions, until noodles are *al dente*.

2. While the pasta is cooking, heat 1 tablespoon of the oil in a large nonstick sauté pan over medium-high heat. Add the chicken; cook, stirring occasionally, for about 2 to 3 minutes or until the chicken is no longer pink on the outside.

3. Reduce the heat to medium; stir in the eggplant, tomatoes, mushrooms, shallots, thyme, and pepper. Cover and cook for about 6 minutes or until the chicken is cooked through and the vegetables are tender. Stir in the vinegar and capers. Adjust the seasoning to taste.

4. When the penne is done, drain well. Return the pasta to the cooking pan. Add the remaining 1 tablespoon of oil; toss.

5. To serve, spoon penne into shallow pasta bowls; top with the chicken-vegetable mixture.

PER SERVING: Cal 265/Prot 20.9g/Carb 23.9g/Fat 9.5g/Chol 63mg/Sod 100mg

Variations

• Substitute other vegetables for the eggplant, tomatoes, or mushrooms (up to 5 cups total). Try cut green beans, red bell pepper strips, sliced zucchini, coarsely chopped artichoke hearts, or oil-packed sun-dried tomatoes, drained and coarsely chopped.

• Rather than serving the chicken-vegetable mixture on pasta, stuff it into pita bread pockets and serve as a warm chicken sandwich.

TIPS

• Eggplant does not necessarily need to be sliced, salted, and weighted to squeeze out the juice. Only overripe eggplant is tough and bitter, so select young, smaller eggplants. The peel is edible, so it is not necessary to peel it. Store eggplant in a plastic bag in the refrigerator for up to 2 weeks.

• Don't wash fresh herbs before storage. Wrap the stem ends with a moist paper towel and refrigerate in a sealed plastic bag. Or place the bunch, stems down, in a glass of water and cover with a plastic bag, securing the bag to the glass with a rubber band; change the water every 2 days. With proper storage, fresh herbs are usable for about 1 week, but for best flavor use them within a few days.

• Dried herbs will remain flavorful for about 1 year when stored in a tightly closed container in a dark, dry place. To get the most out of your dried herbs, crumble them between your fingers as you add them to your recipe to release the aromatic compounds.

• Fresh herbs contain more moisture and are therefore milder in flavor than dried herbs. When substituting, use 3 to 4 times more fresh herbs than dried herbs.

chicken
and **vegetables**
with **penne**

Makes 4 servings

One of the joys of this creation is that it's hearty enough to serve as a meal in itself; another bonus is its versatility. Just follow the basic format and use whatever pasta or vegetables you have on hand.

Dash of salt

8 ounces penne or penne rigate (or about 3 cups); (see Tips)

2 tablespoons olive oil, divided

1 pound boneless skinless chicken breast halves, cut into 1-inch pieces

1 teaspoon minced garlic

2 medium zucchini, halved lengthwise and cut into 1/4-inch-thick slices (about 2 cups)

4 medium scallions, coarsely chopped

6 plum tomatoes, halved lengthwise and cut into 1/4-inch-thick slices (about 3 cups); (see Tips)

1 tablespoon minced fresh basil (or 1 teaspoon dried basil), or to taste

1/2 teaspoon pepper, or to taste

2 teaspoons lemon zest

1 tablespoon fresh lemon juice, or to taste

GARNISH (OPTIONAL)   freshly ground black pepper, freshly grated Parmesan cheese, toasted pine nuts

1.   Bring a large pot of water to a boil over high heat; add salt, then the penne. When the water returns to a boil, stir occasionally to separate the penne. Reduce the heat to medium-high and cook for about 10 to 12 minutes, or according to package istructions, until noodles are *al dente*.

2. While the pasta is cooking, heat 1 tablespoon of the oil in a large nonstick skillet or sauté pan over medium-high heat. Add the chicken; cook, stirring occasionally, for about 4 minutes. Add the garlic; continue cooking for about 1 minute or until the chicken is cooked through and lightly browned.

3. With a slotted spoon, transfer the chicken to a bowl and cover to keep warm.

4. Heat the remaining 1 tablespoon of oil in the skillet; add the zucchini and scallions. Cook, stirring occasionally, for about 4 minutes or until the zucchini is tender. Reduce the heat to low; stir in the chicken, tomatoes, basil, and pepper. Stir gently for about 1 minute or until the tomatoes are softened and the chicken is warm. Remove from the heat; stir in the lemon zest and juice. Adjust the seasonings to taste.

5. When the penne is cooked, drain well. Return the penne to the pot; toss with the chicken-vegetable mixture.

PER SERVING: Cal 338/Prot 37.6g/Carb 21.8g/Fat 11.2g/Chol 106mg/Sod 85mg

ADVANCE PREPARATION   Refrigerate the completed dish and serve chilled later the same day.

Variation

• Substitute other vegetables for the zucchini or tomatoes (up to 5 cups total). Try broccoli florets, cut asparagus, julienned carrots, or oil-packed sun-dried tomatoes, drained and coarsely chopped.

> **TIPS**
>
> • *Rigate* means that the pasta is shaped with ridges, which help the sauce adhere to the surface of the noodles. Shapes such as rotini and rotelle serve the same purpose.
>
> • Plum tomatoes are often called Italian or Roma tomatoes. They have thick, meaty walls, small seeds, little juice, and a rich, sweet flavor. These are the best choice for salads or other recipes that benefit from less juicy tomatoes that retain their shape after being chopped or sliced.

chapter 1 *Stovetop Chicken*

stir-fried
rice
with **chicken**

Makes 4 servings

Rice usually serves a supporting role in a menu; but with the addition of chicken and vegetables, this versatile grain can become a star. In this recipe, you can use white, brown, basmati, or even part or all wild rice. When it comes to vegetables, follow the recipe or use whatever looks good in the market. If available, try exotic mushrooms such as oyster or shiitake.

2 tablespoons canola or safflower oil, divided

12 ounces boneless skinless chicken breast halves, cut into 2-inch-long by $1/2$-inch-wide strips

$1/2$ cup diced carrot

$1/2$ cup diced red bell pepper

1 cup sliced mushrooms (see Tip)

2 medium scallions, finely chopped

1 teaspoon minced garlic

3 cups cooked rice (long-grain white, brown, or basmati)

$1/4$ cup frozen peas (preferably baby peas), thawed

2 tablespoons low-sodium soy sauce, or to taste

Dash of ground white pepper, or to taste

GARNISH (OPTIONAL)   strips of red bell pepper

1. Heat 1 tablespoon of the oil in a large nonstick skillet or wok over medium-high heat. Add the chicken and cook, stirring occasionally, for about 5 minutes or until it is lightly browned and cooked through.

2. With a slotted spoon, transfer the chicken to a bowl and cover to keep warm.

3. Heat the remaining 1 tablespoon of oil in the same pan. Add the carrot and bell pepper; stir-fry for about 2 minutes or until the vegetables are crisp-tender. Add the mushrooms, scallions, and garlic; continue to stir-fry for about 2 minutes or until the vegetables are tender. Add the rice; stir-fry for about 2 minutes.

4. Reduce the heat to low; add the peas, soy sauce, pepper, and the cooked chicken; stir gently until heated through. Adjust the seasonings to taste.

PER SERVING: Cal 376/Protein 30.4g/Carb 39.1g/Fat 10.9g/Chol 65mg/Sod 353mg

ADVANCE PREPARATION   This dish will keep in the refrigerator for up to 2 days; it reheats well.

Variation

• Substitute other vegetables for the carrot, bell pepper, mushrooms, or peas (up to 2$1/2$ cups total). Try cut asparagus, small cauliflower or broccoli florets, diced celery, bok choy, jícama, or water chestnuts.

> **TIP**
>
> There are thousands of varieties of mushrooms. The readily available cultivated white mushroom has a mild, earthy flavor; those labeled "button mushrooms" are immature, smaller white mushrooms. Cremini mushrooms are dark brown, slightly firmer, and have a fuller flavor than their paler relatives; portobello mushrooms are mature creminis. If the mushrooms you buy are sealed in plastic wrap, remove the plastic and place the mushrooms in a paper bag before refrigerating. Before using, brush them with a mushroom brush or wipe with a moist paper towel. If you must rinse them, do so very quickly; because mushrooms are very absorbent, they should not be allowed to soak in water. They also should be cooked quickly; because mushrooms are 90 percent water, overcooking will result in a mushy texture.

chili
rice
with **chicken**

Makes 4 servings

Have it your way: This rice entrée can be pleasantly spicy or seriously fiery, simply by adjusting the amounts of chili powder, jalapeño pepper, and black pepper. Serve it in large, shallow bowls.

1 tablespoon olive oil

12 ounces boneless skinless chicken breast halves, cut into 2-inch-long by 1/4-inch-wide strips

1/2 green bell pepper, coarsely chopped

1/2 red bell pepper, coarsely chopped

1/2 cup minced onion

1 teaspoon minced jalapeño pepper, or to taste (see Tips)

1 teaspoon minced garlic

1 teaspoon chili powder, or to taste

2 teaspoons minced fresh oregano (or 1/2 teaspoon dried oregano)

1/2 teaspoon ground cumin

3 cups cooked rice (long-grain white or brown)

1 (14 1/2-ounce) can diced tomatoes, with juice

1/2 teaspoon pepper, or to taste

1. Heat the oil in a large nonstick skillet over medium-high heat. Add the chicken; cook, stirring occasionally, for about 2 to 3 minutes or until it is no longer pink on the outside. Stir in the bell peppers, onion, jalapeño pepper, garlic, chili powder, dried oregano (if using), and cumin. Cook, stirring occasionally for about 5 minutes or until the vegetables are tender and the chicken is cooked through.

2. Reduce the heat to medium. Stir in the rice, tomatoes with juice, fresh oregano (if using), and pepper. Heat through, stirring occasionally, for about 5 minutes. Adjust the seasonings to taste.

PER SERVING: Cal 356/Prot 29.9g/Carb 41.8g/Fat 7.7g/Chol 65mg/Sod 240mg

ADVANCE PREPARATION   This dish will keep for up to 2 days in the refrigerator and reheats well. The recipe can be successfully doubled or tripled.

Variations

- Add other vegetables (up to 1 cup), such as shredded carrot, chopped celery, cooked sweet corn, or oil-packed sun-dried tomatoes, drained and coarsely chopped (see Tips).

- Stir in one (15-ounce) can beans, drained and rinsed, when you stir in the rice. Try black beans, kidney beans, or garbanzo beans.

- Substitute cooked bulgur wheat for the rice.

TIPS

- Since much of the heat from hot chile peppers comes from the seeds and connecting membranes, remove them for a milder flavor. To avoid irritation from the volatile oils in chile peppers, do not touch your eyes, nose, or lips while handling them. Many cooks wear disposable plastic gloves when working with hot chilies. Afterward, wash your hands, knife, and cutting board in hot, soapy water. To avoid these concerns, try ready-to-use diced chilies, which are available in cans or jars.

- Dried tomatoes must be rehydrated before using in many recipes. Soak them in enough boiling water to cover for about 10 minutes; drain, then use immediately or marinate in olive oil (be sure to refrigerate) for use later.

- Because of their superior flavor and ease of use, I prefer to purchase jars of dried tomatoes that have been rehydrated and packed in olive oil; these, too, must be refrigerated after opening. Drain off the excess oil before using.

chicken, **corn,**
and tomato
skillet

Makes 4 servings

This is pure-and-simple "comfort food"—a nourishing dish that will fill your kitchen with enticing aromas just as if you'd been cooking all day. (Would you believe 15 minutes?)

1 cup chicken broth

1 (14$\frac{1}{2}$-ounce) can diced tomatoes, with juice

8 ounces boneless skinless chicken breast halves, cut into $\frac{1}{2}$-inch pieces

$\frac{2}{3}$ cup basmati rice (see Tips)

1 cup frozen corn

2 tablespoons minced fresh basil (or 1 teaspoon dried basil)

$\frac{1}{2}$ teaspoon pepper, or to taste

GARNISH (OPTIONAL)   freshly grated Parmesan cheese (see Tips), sprigs of fresh basil

1. Stir together the chicken broth and tomatoes with juice in a large nonstick sauté pan. Bring the mixture to a boil over high heat.

2. Stir in the chicken, rice, corn, dried basil (if using), and pepper. When the liquid returns to a boil, reduce the heat to medium; cover, and cook for about 12 minutes or until the chicken is cooked through and the rice is done. Stir in the fresh basil (if using). Adjust the seasoning to taste.

PER SERVING: Cal 264/Prot 22.1g/Carb 38g/Fat 2.6g/Chol 44mg/Sod 400mg

ADVANCE PREPARATION   This dish can be made in advance, refrigerated, and reheated within 2 days. The rice (or bulgur wheat; see Variations) will absorb some of the moisture, so add some tomato sauce or tomato juice when reheating.

Variations

- Substitute $^2/_3$ cup uncooked bulgur wheat for the rice.

- Substitute summer savory or oregano for the basil.

- Add up to $^1/_4$ cup oil-packed sun-dried tomatoes, drained and coarsely chopped.

- For a spicier flavor, add red pepper flakes to taste.

TIPS

- Basmati, the most famous aromatic rice, is grown in the foothills of the Himalaya Mountains; less aromatic varieties are grown in the United States, primarily in the Southwest and California. In both brown and white forms, it has a nutlike fragrance while cooking and a delicate, almost-buttery flavor. Lower in starch than other long-grain rices, basmati rice grains cook up flaky and separate. Best of all, basmati rice can be prepared in just 15 minutes.

- Always buy freshly grated Parmesan cheese, or grate your own from a block of Parmesan using a hand grater or a food processor. Sealed in a tightly closed container, freshly grated Parmesan will keep in the refrigerator for up to 1 week; it can be frozen, although the flavor and texture deteriorate. Wrapped tightly in plastic wrap, a block of Parmesan cheese will keep for up to 2 to 4 weeks in the refrigerator.

chicken
and mushroom
risotto

Makes 4 servings

Arborio rice is an Italian short-grain rice, which can be found in the rice section or among the ethnic foods in most supermarkets and specialty stores. It is the ideal rice for risotto, Spanish paella, and rice puddings because the plentiful starch in its grains imparts a creamy texture when cooked.

1 (14-ounce) can chicken broth (2 cups)	1 cup sliced mushrooms
3 cups water	2 tablespoons minced shallot
2 tablespoons olive oil, divided	1 cup Arborio rice (see Tip)
8 ounces boneless skinless chicken breast halves, cut into 2-inch-long by $1/2$-inch-wide strips	$1/2$ cup freshly grated Parmesan cheese
	$1/2$ teaspoon pepper, or to taste

GARNISH (OPTIONAL)   freshly ground black pepper, sprigs of fresh flat-leaf parsley

1. Stir together the chicken broth and water in a small saucepan. Bring the mixture to a boil over high heat. Cover and reduce the heat to medium, or to a temperature high enough to maintain a simmer.

2. Meanwhile, heat 1 tablespoon of the oil in a medium nonstick skillet over medium-high heat. Add the chicken, mushrooms, and shallot; cook, stirring occasionally, for about 4 minutes or until the chicken is almost cooked through. Remove the pan from the heat, cover, and set aside.

3. While the chicken is cooking, heat the remaining 1 tablespoon of oil in a large non-stick sauté pan over medium-high heat. Add the rice; stir for about 2 minutes or until

each grain is coated with oil. Pour 1 cup of the simmering broth mixture into the skillet (maintain a cooking temperature high enough so that the hot broth continues bubbling after it is added to the rice). Cook, stirring constantly, for about 3 minutes or until the liquid is absorbed.

4. Stir the chicken-mushroom mixture into the rice. Add the hot broth 1 cup at a time, stirring constantly. Add another cup of hot broth only after the previous cup has been absorbed. Continue until the rice is tender but still firm. (You may not need to use all 5 cups of the broth mixture.) This process will take about 10 minutes.

5. Remove the pan from the heat; add the Parmesan and pepper, stirring until the cheese is melted into the rice. Adjust the seasoning to taste.

PER SERVING: Cal 391/Prot 27.9g/Carb 39.8g/Fat 13.3g/Chol 53mg/Sod 665mg

ADVANCE PREPARATION   Risotto tastes best when served immediately, but this dish be refrigerated and served the next day. To reheat, add a little water and stir gently over low heat, or microwave at medium for about 2 minutes.

> ### TIP
>
> To reach the correct consistency for risotto, the rice must be first sautéed, and hot liquid must be added gradually, stirring continually while it cooks; more liquid is added when each addition of liquid is absorbed. Maintaining the correct cooking temperature is important, because the mixture should remain bubbly. If the heat is too high, the rice will absorb the broth too quickly and will not cook evenly. If the heat is too low, the broth will be absorbed too slowly, resulting in a gluey consistency.

Variations

- Substitute 1 cup white wine for 1 cup of the water.

- Substitute other vegetables for part of the mushrooms (up to 1¹/₂ cups total). Try red bell pepper strips, steamed cut asparagus, or oil-packed sun-dried tomatoes, drained and coarsely chopped.

- Stir in 2 tablespoons Basil Pesto (page 97) with the Parmesan cheese.

- Add 1 teaspoon dried or 1 tablespoon minced fresh herbs, such as basil or rosemary, with the Parmesan cheese.

chicken and vegetable
stir-fry
with ginger sauce

Makes 4 servings

Serve this stir-fry over rice or Chinese wheat-flour noodles.

Ginger Sauce

6 tablespoons white rice vinegar

6 tablespoons sugar

$^3/_4$ cup water

2 tablespoons low-sodium soy sauce

1 tablespoon cold water

1 tablespoon cornstarch

1 tablespoon finely minced fresh ginger (see Tips)

To Complete the Recipe

2 tablespoons canola or safflower oil, divided

12 ounces boneless skinless chicken breast halves, cut into 2-inch-long by $^1/_2$-inch-wide strips

3 ribs bok choy, cut into $^1/_4$-inch slices (also shred green tops)

2 carrots, thinly sliced diagonally

1 red bell pepper, cut into 2-inch-long by $^3/_8$-inch-wide strips

1 small onion, thinly sliced (about $^1/_2$ cup)

1 teaspoon minced garlic

GARNISH (OPTIONAL)   toasted sesame seeds, toasted sliced almonds, mandarin orange segments, scallion curls (see Tips, page 17)

1. To prepare the sauce, stir together the vinegar, sugar, $^3/_4$ cup water, and soy sauce in a small saucepan. Bring the mixture to a boil over medium-high heat; reduce the heat to low, and simmer, stirring occasionally, for 2 minutes.

2. Meanwhile, stir together the cold water and the cornstarch in a small bowl or measuring cup until smooth; stir into the saucepan. Cook, stirring constantly, until the sauce is clear and slightly thickened. Remove the pan from the heat; stir in the ginger and cover.

3. To prepare the stir-fry, heat 1 tablespoon of the canola or safflower oil in a large skillet or wok over medium-high heat. Add the chicken and stir-fry for about 5 minutes or until it is cooked through.

4. With a slotted spoon, transfer the chicken to a bowl and cover to keep warm.

5. Heat the remaining 1 tablespoon of canola or safflower oil in the pan. Stir-fry the bok choy, carrots, bell pepper, and onion for about 4 minutes or until the vegetables are crisp-tender. Stir the garlic and the cooked chicken.

6. Serve mounds of the stir-fry mixture atop rice or Chinese wheat-flour noodles. Drizzle each serving with about $^1/_4$ cup of the sauce.

PER SERVING: Cal 312/Prot 26.5g/Carb 30g/Fat 9.6g/Chol 65mg/Sod 373mg

ADVANCE PREPARATION   The ginger sauce can be made up to 2 days in advance and reheated. Serve with freshly stir-fried chicken and vegetables.

Variation

• Substitute other vegetables for the bok choy, carrots, and bell pepper (up to 5 cups total). Try broccoli florets, sliced mushrooms, sliced zucchini, stemmed snow peas, or shredded Chinese cabbage. With the cooked chicken, stir in peas, baby corn ears, wedges of plum tomatoes, or water chestnuts; stir gently until heated through.

TIPS

• When buying fresh ginger, look for firm, irregularly shaped rhizomes with smooth brown skin and no soft spots. Store at room temperature and use within a few days.

• To preserve ginger, peel and cut it into chunks, place in a jar, and add sherry to cover. Cap the jar and refrigerate. Ginger can be stored in this way for several months. For even longer storage, wrap the ginger tightly in aluminum foil and freeze. When you need ginger, without thawing, grate off the amount needed; rewrap and refreeze. Frozen ginger will keep for up to 3 months.

• Jars of preminced ginger are available in most produce departments. Dried ginger does not equate with fresh in Asian recipes.

chapter 1 *Stovetop Chicken*

cashew
chicken
stir-fry

Makes 4 servings

Here's a Chinese classic best served with a plentiful amount of hot rice. Make the dish spicy or keep it mild by adjusting the amount of red pepper flakes in the sauce.

Spicy Sauce

1 tablespoon cold water

1 tablespoon cornstarch

1 cup chicken broth

2 tablespoons low-sodium soy sauce

2 teaspoons minced garlic

$1/2$ teaspoon red pepper flakes, or to taste (see Tips)

$1/2$ teaspoon powdered turmeric

Dash of ground white pepper, or to taste

To Complete the Recipe

2 tablespoons canola or safflower oil, divided

12 ounces boneless skinless chicken breast halves, cut into 2-inch-long by $1/2$-inch-wide strips

4 cups broccoli florets

1 large red bell pepper, cut into 2-inch-long by $1/4$-inch-wide strips

3 medium scallions, cut into $1 1/2$-inch strips

$1/4$ cup whole raw cashews (see Tips)

1. To prepare the sauce, stir together the water and cornstarch in a small bowl or 2-cup measure until smooth. Stir in the remaining sauce ingredients; set aside.

2. To prepare the stir-fry, heat 1 tablespoon of the oil in large skillet or wok over medium-high heat. Add the chicken and stir-fry for about 5 minutes or until it is lightly browned and cooked through.

3. With a slotted spoon, transfer the chicken to a bowl and cover to keep warm.

4. Heat the remaining 1 tablespoon of oil in the same pan. Add the broccoli; stir-fry for about 2 minutes. Add the bell pepper and scallions; continue to stir-fry for about 3 minutes or until the broccoli and bell pepper are crisp-tender.

5. Reduce the heat to medium. Stir the sauce and pour it over the vegetables. Cook, stirring constantly, for about 30 seconds or until the sauce becomes clear and thickens slightly. Stir in the chicken and cashews. Adjust the seasonings to taste.

6. To serve, spoon a bed of rice onto individual serving plates. Top with the stir-fry mixture.

PER SERVING: Cal 301/Prot 30.9g/Carb 12.5g/Fat 14.1g/Chol 65mg/Sod 540mg

Variations

- Substitute other vegetables for the broccoli or bell pepper (up to 5 cups total). Try cut asparagus, sliced celery or bok choy, julienned carrots, water chestnuts, or stemmed snow peas.

- Substitute pine nuts for the cashews.

> ## TIPS
>
> - Red pepper flakes, also called crushed red pepper, are the seeds and flakes of fiery hot peppers; a small amount goes a long way! Refrigerate to preserve the color and flavor.
>
> - For cooking, raw cashews are preferable to roasted and salted cashews. With no added salt or fat, raw cashews will absorb the other flavors in your recipe. They soften and plump slightly to a pleasing consistency.

chicken
with **sweet peppers**
and balsamic sauce

Makes 4 servings

Balsamic vinegar elevates the mundane sweet-and-sour combination to magnificent. This chicken and vegetable combination is at its best spooned over rice or egg noodles.

Balsamic Sauce

1 tablespoon cold water

1 tablespoon cornstarch

1 cup chicken broth

1/2 cup balsamic vinegar (see Tip)

1 teaspoon sugar, or to taste (if a lower grade, more acidic balsamic vinegar is used, more sugar may be necessary)

1/2 teaspoon pepper, or to taste

To Complete the Recipe

3 tablespoons all-purpose flour

1/2 teaspoon paprika

Dash of salt, or to taste

12 ounces boneless skinless chicken breast halves, cut into 1-inch-wide lengthwise strips

2 tablespoons olive oil, divided

1 red bell pepper, cut into 3/8-inch-wide lengthwise strips

1 yellow bell pepper, cut into 3/8-inch-wide lengthwise strips

1 teaspoon minced garlic

1/4 cup raisins

1/4 cup minced fresh flat-leaf parsley

GARNISH (OPTIONAL)   freshly ground black pepper, toasted sliced almonds

1. To prepare the sauce, stir together the water and cornstarch in a small bowl until smooth. Add the remaining sauce ingredients, stirring until the sugar is dissolved; set aside.

2. To prepare the chicken, combine the flour, paprika, and salt in a shallow bowl. Flour the chicken by lightly pressing both sides of each chicken strip into the flour mixture.

3. Heat 1 tablespoon of the oil in a large nonstick sauté pan over medium-high heat. Arrange the chicken strips in a single layer; cook for about 2 minutes on each side or until they are lightly browned but not cooked through.

4. With tongs, transfer the chicken to a plate and cover to keep warm.

5. Heat the remaining 1 tablespoon of oil in the sauté pan. Add the bell peppers and garlic. Cook, stirring, for about 3 minutes or until the peppers are crisp-tender. Stir the sauce and pour it into the skillet; cook, stirring, for about 1 minute or until the sauce becomes clear and thickens slightly.

6. Reduce the heat to medium and stir in the chicken. Cover and cook for about 8 minutes or until the chicken is thoroughly done. Stir in the raisins and parsley during the last couple of minutes. Adjust the seasonings to taste.

PER SERVING: Cal 292/Prot 27.1g/Carb 23.6g/Fat 9.9g/Chol 65mg/Sod 291mg

TIP

Balsamic vinegar (the Italian *aceto balsamico*) is an Italian red wine vinegar made by boiling the juice of white Trebbiano grapes in copper pots until it caramelizes. It is then aged for 3 to 30 years in barrels made from various woods (oak, chestnut, mulberry, and juniper), each adding a hint of its woody flavor. The result is a vinegar with a heavy, mellow, almost-sweet flavor and a dark color. Store balsamic vinegar in a cool, dark place for up to 6 months after it has been opened.

chicken
with black bean–
tomato sauce

Makes 4 servings

Most of these ingredients are staples that you probably have on hand. Rice and a green salad make the meal complete.

3 tablespoons all-purpose flour

$1/8$ teaspoon pepper

12 ounces boneless skinless chicken breast halves, cut into 1-inch-wide lengthwise strips

1 tablespoon olive oil

Black Bean–Tomato Sauce

1 tablespoon olive oil

$1/2$ green bell pepper, coarsely chopped

$1/4$ cup coarsely chopped onion

1 (15-ounce) can black beans, drained and rinsed (see Tip)

1 ($14^1/2$-ounce) can diced tomatoes, with juice

1 (4-ounce) can diced green chilies, drained

$1/2$ cup frozen corn

$1/2$ teaspoon pepper, or to taste

2 tablespoons minced fresh cilantro, or to taste (or 2 tablespoons minced fresh basil or oregano)

2 tablespoons fresh lime juice

GARNISH (OPTIONAL)   freshly ground black pepper and sprigs of fresh cilantro, basil, or oregano

1. To prepare the chicken, combine the flour and pepper in a shallow bowl. Flour the chicken by lightly pressing both sides of each chicken strip into the flour mixture.

2. Heat the oil in a large nonstick sauté pan over medium-high heat. Arrange the chicken strips in a single layer; cook for about 2 minutes on each side or until they are lightly browned but not cooked through.

3. With tongs, transfer the chicken to a plate and cover to keep warm.

4. To prepare the sauce, heat the oil in the sauté pan over medium-high heat. Add the bell pepper and onion; cook, stirring occasionally, for about 3 minutes or until crisp-tender. Stir in the beans, tomatoes with juice, green chilies, corn, pepper, and dried basil or oregano (if using).

5. Reduce the heat to medium and stir in the chicken. Cover and cook for about 8 minutes or until the chicken is thoroughly done. Stir in the fresh cilantro, basil, or oregano (if using) and the lime juice. Adjust the seasoning to taste.

PER SERVING: Cal 398/Prot 36.5g/Carb 39.5g/Fat 10.4g/Chol 65mg/Sod 638mg

Variations

•   Substitute other vegetables for part or all of the green bell pepper (up to $^1/_2$ cup total). Try coarsely chopped red bell pepper or oil-packed sun-dried tomatoes, drained and coarsely chopped.

•   For a hotter flavor, add minced jalapeño peppers, red pepper flakes, or a dash of hot pepper sauce to taste.

> ### TIP
>
> Black beans, also called turtle beans or *frijoles negros,* are a member of the kidney bean family. Black on the outside, cream-colored within, they keep their shape and sweet, hearty flavor after cooking. Canned black beans are available in most supermarkets.

with **chicken**
roasted
sweet red pepper sauce

Makes 4 servings

Roasted red bell peppers are found in the condiment section of most supermarkets; Cajun seasoning is in the spice section. When time permits, you can roast your own peppers, and packaged Cajun seasoning can be replaced with homemade Cajun Seasoning Mix (page 47). When in season, corn on the cob is my favorite accompaniment for this dish; and, of course, rice always makes a good choice.

Roasted Sweet Red Pepper Sauce

1 (12-ounce) jar roasted red bell peppers, drained (about 1¾ cups), or 3 freshly roasted red bell peppers (see Tip)

¼ cup water

2 tablespoons fresh lime juice

1 tablespoon olive oil

1 tablespoon minced onion

2 teaspoons Cajun Seasoning Mix, or to taste, or 2 teaspoons packaged Cajun seasoning

½ teaspoon minced garlic

½ teaspoon pepper, or to taste

To Complete the Recipe

4 boneless skinless chicken breast halves (about 4 ounces each)

3 tablespoons all-purpose flour

⅛ teaspoon pepper, or to taste

1 tablespoon olive oil

GARNISH (OPTIONAL) sprigs of fresh flat-leaf parsley

1. To prepare the sauce, process all of the ingredients in a food processor or blender until smooth. Adjust the seasoning to taste; set aside.

2. To prepare the chicken, place the chicken breasts between 2 sheets of plastic wrap or place in a plastic bag; flatten them to a ¹/₂-inch uniform thickness.

3. Combine the flour and pepper in a shallow bowl. Flour the chicken by lightly pressing both sides of each chicken breast into the flour mixture.

4. Heat the oil in a large nonstick sauté pan over medium-high heat. Arrange the chicken breasts in a single layer; cook for about 2 minutes on each side or until they are lightly browned but not cooked through.

5. Reduce the heat to medium and pour the sauce over the chicken breasts. Cover and cook for about 8 minutes or until the chicken is thoroughly done. Adjust the seasoning to taste.

6. To serve, transfer the chicken breasts to serving plates and top with the roasted red pepper sauce.

PER SERVING: Cal 260/Protein 33.9g/Carb 7.8g/Fat 10.4g/Chol 87mg/Sod 72mg

> **TIP**
>
> To roast fresh peppers, adjust the oven rack to about 3 inches from the heating element; preheat the broiler. Cut the peppers in half lengthwise; discard the stems, seeds, and membranes. Place the peppers, skin sides up, on a foil-lined baking sheet; flatten each with the palm of your hand. Broil for about 5 minutes or until the skins are blackened, charred, and blistered. Transfer the peppers to a zip-top, heavy-duty, plastic bag or small paper bag, and seal; set aside for about 10 minutes or until cool. (The steam will loosen the skin.) Remove the pepper halves from the bag; peel and discard the skins.

cajun
seasoning mix

Makes ¹/₄ cup

1¹/₂ tablespoons paprika

1 tablespoon dried thyme

1 teaspoon dried basil

1 teaspoon dried oregano

1 teaspoon pepper

1 teaspoon cayenne pepper

Dash of salt

1. Shake all of the ingredients together in a small covered glass jar.

2. Store in an airtight container in a cool, dark place for up to 6 months.

autumn
chicken
and **pears**

Makes 4 servings

Pears join cranberries in the perfect entrée to welcome autumn. For another salute to fall, try the apple variation. Aromatic basmati rice is the ideal accompaniment.

4 boneless skinless chicken breast halves (about 4 ounces each)

3 tablespoons all-purpose flour

1/8 teaspoon pepper

Dash of salt

2 tablespoons olive oil, divided

2 pears (at room temperature), peeled if desired, cored and cut into 1/4-inch wedges

2 medium scallions, finely chopped

1/2 teaspoon minced garlic

3/4 cup apple juice

1/4 cup dried cranberries

1 tablespoon fresh thyme leaves (or 1 teaspoon dried thyme)

1/2 teaspoon pepper, or to taste (see Tips)

GARNISH (OPTIONAL)   toasted sliced almonds, coarsely chopped pecans or walnuts

1. Place the chicken breasts between 2 sheets of plastic wrap or in a plastic bag; flatten them to a 1/2-inch uniform thickness.

2. Combine the flour, 1/8 teaspoon pepper, and salt in a shallow bowl. Flour the chicken by lightly pressing both sides of each chicken breast into the flour mixture.

3. Heat 1 tablespoon of the oil in a large nonstick sauté pan over medium-high heat. Arrange the chicken breasts in a single layer; cook for about 2 minutes on each side or until they are lightly browned but not cooked through.

4. With tongs, transfer the chicken to a plate and cover to keep warm.

5. Heat the remaining 1 tablespoon of olive oil in the sauté pan. Add the pears, scallions, and garlic. Cook, stirring, for about 2 minutes or until the pears are slightly tender.

6. Reduce the heat to medium. Stir in the remaining ingredients and return the chicken to the skillet. Cover and cook for about 8 minutes or until the chicken is thoroughly done. Adjust the seasoning to taste.

7. For each serving, place a chicken breast on a bed of rice or couscous; top with the pears, cranberries, and sauce.

PER SERVING: Cal 320/Prot 33.7g/Carb 22.4g/Fat 10.6g/Chol 87mg/Sod 72mg

Variations

• Substitute other fruit for the 2 pears. Try 2 apples, or 1 pear and 1 apple.

• Substitute other fruit for the dried cranberries. Try currants or raisins.

TIPS

• Berries of the pepper vine are used to produce both black pepper and white pepper. For black pepper, green berries are picked and sun-dried, turning black and shrinking in the process. For white pepper, the berries are allowed to ripen on the vine; they are picked and soaked in water to remove the outer coating, leaving the inner gray-white kernel. The inner kernels are sun-dried to produce white pepper.

• Freshly ground, whole dried peppercorns are more flavorful than preground pepper, because, once cracked, the pepper releases much of its oil. The best pepper grinders have settings for both coarse and fine grinds. To measure, grind the pepper onto a sheet of waxed paper and pour into a measuring spoon.

orange-kahlua
chicken

Makes 4 servings

This dish never fails to excite the palate with a touch of citrus and a hint of coffee flavor.

Orange-Kahlua Sauce

$^3/_4$ cup fresh orange juice (see Tip)

$^1/_3$ cup Kahlua

1 teaspoon orange zest

To Complete the Recipe

3 tablespoons all-purpose flour

$^1/_8$ teaspoon pepper

Dash of salt

1 pound boneless skinless chicken breast halves, cut into 1-inch-wide lengthwise strips

1 tablespoon olive oil

TIP

To squeeze more juice from lemons, limes, and oranges, first bring them to room temperature. Then roll the fruit around on a hard surface, pressing hard with the palm of your hand, before cutting and squeezing.

---

1. To prepare the sauce, stir the ingredients in a small bowl or measuring cup; set aside.

2. To prepare the chicken, combine the flour, pepper, and salt in a shallow bowl. Flour the chicken by lightly pressing both sides of each chicken strip into the flour mixture.

3. Heat the oil in a large nonstick sauté pan over medium-high heat. Arrange the chicken strips in a single layer; cook for about 2 minutes on each side or until they are lightly browned but not cooked through.

4. Reduce the heat to medium. Stir the sauce and pour it over the chicken. Cover and cook for about 8 minutes, turning once, until the chicken is thoroughly done.

5. To serve, transfer the chicken strips to serving plates with rice, and drizzle with the sauce.

PER SERVING: Cal 273/Prot 33.6g/Carb 18.8g/Fat 7g/Chol 87mg/Sod 73mg

braised
chicken
with papaya

Makes 4 servings

This tropical chicken dish is one of the simplest of all to prepare. It's also one of my favorites, especially when paired with basmati rice.

3 tablespoons all-purpose flour

$^1/_8$ teaspoon pepper

1 pound boneless skinless chicken breast halves, cut into 1-inch-wide lengthwise strips

1 tablespoon olive oil

1 (10$^1/_2$-ounce) can chicken broth (1$^1/_4$ cups)

1 large papaya (at room temperature), peeled, halved lengthwise, seeded, and cut into $^1/_2$-inch-thick slices

GARNISH (OPTIONAL)   freshly ground black pepper, sprigs of fresh cilantro

1. Combine the flour and pepper in a shallow bowl. Flour the chicken by lightly pressing both sides of each chicken strip into the flour mixture.

2. Heat the oil in a large nonstick sauté pan over medium-high heat. Arrange the chicken strips in a single layer; cook for about 2 minutes on each side or until they are lightly browned but not cooked through.

3. Reduce the heat to medium and pour the chicken broth over the chicken. Place the papaya slices atop the chicken. Cover and cook for about 8 minutes or until the chicken is thoroughly done.

4. To serve, spread a mound of rice on each of 4 plates. Top with the chicken strips and papaya slices; drizzle with the chicken broth.

PER SERVING: Cal 241/Prot 35.1g/Carb 8.5g/Fat 7.4g/Chol 87mg/Sod 315mg

chicken and grapes
in blush wine
sauce

Makes 4 servings

As the chicken cooks, a lovely sauce forms in the pan. Enjoy every bit of it by spooning it over the chicken and grapes. Serve atop couscous, or rice if you prefer.

Blush Wine Sauce

1 tablespoon cold water

1 tablespoon cornstarch

1 cup blush wine (see Tip)

$1/2$ cup chicken broth

$1/2$ teaspoon pepper, or to taste

1 teaspoon minced fresh rosemary (or $1/4$ teaspoon dried rosemary, crushed)

To Complete the Recipe

3 tablespoons all-purpose flour

$1/2$ teaspoon paprika

$1/8$ teaspoon pepper

1 pound boneless skinless chicken breast halves, cut into 1-inch-wide lengthwise strips

1 tablespoon olive oil

2 tablespoons minced shallot

1 cup halved seedless red or green grapes (at room temperature)

GARNISH (OPTIONAL)   freshly ground black pepper, sprigs of fresh parsley

1. To prepare the sauce, stir together the water and cornstarch in a small bowl or a 2-cup measure until smooth. Stir in the remaining ingredients; set aside.

2. To prepare the chicken, combine the flour, paprika, and pepper in a shallow bowl. Flour the chicken by lightly pressing both sides of each chicken strip into the flour mixture.

3. Heat the oil in a large nonstick sauté pan over medium-high heat. Stir in the shallot. Arrange the chicken strips in a single layer; cook for about 2 minutes on each side or until the chicken strips are lightly browned but not cooked through.

4. Reduce the heat to medium. Stir the sauce and pour it over the chicken. Cover and cook for about 8 minutes or until the chicken is thoroughly done. Adjust the seasoning to taste.

5. Reduce the heat to low; stir in the grapes. Cover and allow the mixture to heat for about 1 minute or until the grapes are warmed through.

6. For each serving, arrange the strips of chicken on a bed of couscous or rice, top with cooked grapes, and drizzle with the sauce.

> **TIP**
>
> Blush wines are usually made from red grapes, but because the skins and stems are removed early in the wine-making process, the color becomes light pink (or rose). In general, blush wines are very light-bodied and slightly sweet. In the United States, "blush" has generally replaced the term "rosé."

PER SERVING: Cal 268/Prot 34.8g/Carb 15.7g/Fat 7.3g/Chol 87mg/Sod 174mg

Variations

• Substitute dry white wine for the blush wine.

• Substitute ¼ teaspoon dried thyme and ¼ teaspoon dried oregano for the rosemary.

chicken
marsala
on egg noodles

Makes 4 servings

Portobello mushrooms, shallots, and Marsala wine can be pricey ingredients, but their distinctive flavors, intoxicating aromas, and elegance are worth the extra cost. Serve this dish to your most discriminating guests.

Marsala Sauce

1 tablespoon cold water

2 teaspoons cornstarch

1$^1/_4$ cups sweet Marsala wine (see Tips)

$^1/_4$ cup fresh lemon juice

$^1/_8$ teaspoon pepper, or to taste

To Complete the Recipe

3 tablespoons all-purpose flour

$^1/_8$ teaspoon pepper

Dash of salt

1 pound boneless skinless chicken breast halves, cut into 1-inch-wide lengthwise strips

2 tablespoons olive oil, divided

3 portobello mushroom caps, cut into $^1/_2$-inch-wide slices (see Tips)

$^1/_4$ cup minced shallots

8 ounces wide egg noodles (about 4 cups)

GARNISH (OPTIONAL)   freshly ground black pepper, thin lemon slices, sprigs of fresh flat-leaf parsley

1. Begin heating a large pot of water over high heat for the noodles.

2. While the water is coming to a boil, prepare the sauce: Stir together the water and cornstarch in a small bowl until smooth. Stir in the remaining sauce ingredients; set aside.

3. To prepare the chicken, combine the flour, pepper, and salt in a shallow bowl. Flour the chicken by lightly pressing both sides of each chicken strip into the flour mixture.

4. Heat 1 tablespoon of the oil in a large nonstick sauté pan over medium-high heat. Arrange the chicken strips in a single layer; cook for about 2 minutes on each side or until they are lightly browned but not cooked through.

5. With tongs, transfer the chicken to a plate and cover to keep warm.

6. Heat the remaining 1 tablespoon of oil in the sauté pan over medium heat. Add the mushrooms and shallots; cook, stirring and turning the mushrooms occasionally, for about 3 minutes or until the mushrooms are lightly browned but not tender. Stir the sauce and pour it over the mushrooms; cook, stirring constantly, for about 1 minute or until the sauce becomes clear and thickens slightly.

7. Stir in the chicken. Cover and cook for about 8 minutes or until the chicken is thoroughly done. Adjust the seasoning to taste.

8. While the chicken is cooking, add salt, then the noodles to the boiling water. When the water returns to a boil, stir occasionally to separate the noodles. Reduce the heat to medium-high and cook for about 5 to 7 minutes, or according to package instructions, until the noodles are tender; drain well.

9. Spoon a bed of noodles onto 4 plates. Top with chicken-mushroom mixture; drizzle with the sauce.

PER SERVING: Cal 494/Prot 42.5g/Carb 52.3g/Fat 12.8g/Chol 141mg/Sod 87mg

TIPS

- The best Marsala wine is imported from Sicily. It has a rich, smoky flavor that can range from sweet to dry. Like port, sherry, and other dessert wines, Marsala is a "fortified" wine, which means brandy or another spirit has been added, increasing the alcohol content and enhancing the flavor.

- Portobello mushrooms are large, dark brown mushrooms with an open, flat cap; the tops can easily measure 6 inches in diameter. Because of long growing cycles, the portobello gills are fully exposed, which means that some of the moisture has evaporated. This concentrates and enriches the flavor and creates a dense, meaty texture.

lemon-caper
chicken
on
capellini

Makes 4 servings

Accompanied by crusty bread and a crisp green salad, this dish saves the day when time is short and special guests are on the way.

Lemon-Caper Sauce

1 tablespoon cold water

1 tablespoon cornstarch

1 (10^1/$_2$-ounce) can chicken broth (1^1/$_4$ cups)

^{1}/$_4$ cup fresh lemon juice

1 teaspoon lemon zest

^{1}/$_2$ teaspoon ·pepper, or to taste

1 tablespoon capers, drained and rinsed (see Tip)

To Complete the Recipe

3 tablespoons all-purpose flour

^{1}/$_8$ teaspoon pepper

Dash of salt

1 pound boneless skinless chicken breast halves, cut into 1-inch-wide lengthwise strips

2 tablespoons olive oil, divided

2 cups asparagus in 2-inch-long pieces (2 cups)

2 medium scallions, cut into 2-inch lengthwise strips

1 teaspoon minced garlic

8 ounces capellini pasta

GARNISH (OPTIONAL)   snipped fresh chives, lemon slices

1. Begin heating a large pot of water over high heat for the capellini.

2. While the water is coming to a boil, prepare the sauce: Stir together the water and cornstarch in a small bowl or 2-cup measure until smooth. Stir in the remaining sauce ingredients; set aside.

3. To prepare the chicken, combine the flour, pepper, and salt in a shallow bowl. Flour the chicken by lightly pressing both sides of each chicken strip into the flour mixture.

4. Heat 1 tablespoon of the oil in a large nonstick sauté pan over medium-high heat. Arrange the chicken strips in a single layer; cook for about 2 minutes on each side or until they are lightly browned but not cooked through.

5. With tongs, transfer the chicken to a plate and cover to keep warm.

6. Heat the remaining 1 tablespoon of oil in the sauté pan. Add the asparagus; cook for about 3 minutes, stirring occasionally. Add the scallions and garlic; cook, stirring occasionally, for about 2 more minutes or until the asparagus is tender.

7. Stir the sauce and pour it into the skillet; cook, stirring, for about 1 minute or until the sauce becomes clear and thickens slightly.

8. Reduce the heat to medium and stir in the chicken. Cover and cook for about 8 minutes or until the chicken is thoroughly done. Adjust the seasoning to taste.

9. While the chicken is cooking, add salt, then the capellini to the boiling water. When the water returns to a boil, stir occasionally to separate the capellini. Reduce the heat to medium-high and cook for about 5 to 7 minutes, or according to package instructions, until *al dente*; drain well.

10. To assemble the servings, arrange a bed of capellini on each of 4 plates. Top with chicken strips and vegetables; drizzle with the sauce.

> **TIP**
>
> Capers are the unopened flower buds of a shrub native to the Mediterranean and parts of Asia. The buds are dried in the sun and then pickled in a vinegar brine. Capers come in several sizes; the largest have the strongest flavor. The smallest, called "non-pareil," are subtle in taste but are the most tender and most expensive. Capers should be rinsed before using to remove excess salt. Once opened, store in the refrigerator for up to 2 or 3 months.

PER SERVING: Cal 367/Prot 40.3g/Carb 25.4g/Fat 11.6g/Chol 106mg/Sod 347mg

Variation

- Substitute sliced mushrooms for all or part of the asparagus (up to 2 cups total).

Chicken with Linguine and Tomato-Basil Sauce

chicken
with linguine
and tomato-basil sauce

Makes 4 servings

The secret to the success of this simple recipe is using top-quality ingredients. Canned diced tomatoes are a time-saver and a far better choice than mediocre fresh tomatoes. Use fresh garlic, fresh basil, freshly ground pepper, and extra-virgin olive oil. If available, select chicken "tenders" rather than chicken breast halves.

Tomato-Basil Sauce

1 (14^1/$_2$-ounce) can diced tomatoes, with juice

2 teaspoons minced garlic

3 tablespoons minced fresh basil (or 1 tablespoon dried basil)

^{1}/$_2$ teaspoon pepper, or to taste

Dash of salt, or to taste

To Complete the Recipe

3 tablespoons all-purpose flour

^{1}/$_4$ teaspoon pepper

Dash of salt

12 ounces boneless skinless chicken breast halves, cut into 3-inch-long by 1-inch-wide strips

2 tablespoons extra-virgin olive oil, divided (see Tips)

8 ounces linguine

GARNISH (OPTIONAL)   freshly ground black pepper, freshly grated Parmesan cheese, chèvre cheese, toasted pine nuts, sprigs of fresh basil

1. Begin heating a large pot of salted water over high heat for the linguine.

2. While the water is coming to a boil, prepare the sauce: Stir together the tomatoes with juice, garlic, dried basil (if using), pepper, and salt in a medium bowl; set aside.

59

(continues)

3. To prepare the chicken, combine the flour, pepper, and salt in a shallow bowl. Flour the chicken by lightly pressing both sides of each chicken strip into the flour mixture.

4. Heat 1 tablespoon of the olive oil in a large nonstick sauté pan over medium-high heat. Arrange the chicken strips in a single layer; cook for about 2 minutes on each side or until they are lightly browned but not cooked through.

5. Reduce the heat to medium; pour the sauce over the chicken. Cover and cook for about 8 minutes or until the chicken is thoroughly done. Add the fresh basil (if using) during the last minute or two. Adjust the seasonings to taste.

6. While the chicken is cooking, add salt, then the linguine to the boiling water. When the water returns to a boil, stir occasionally to separate the linguine. Reduce the heat to medium-high and cook for about 8 to 10 minutes, or according to package instructions, until noodles are *al dente*; drain well. Return the pasta to the pan and toss with the remaining 1 tablespoon of oil.

7. For each serving, in a large shallow bowl arrange chicken strips on a bed of linguine; top with the sauce.

PER SERVING: Cal 299/Prot 29.1g/Carb 22.7g/Fat 10.2g/Chol 84mg/Sod 224mg

TIPS

- Extra-virgin olive oil is made from the first pressing of top-quality olives. The oil has a pronounced, full-bodied, fruity taste and low acidity. The color and fragrance vary depending upon the variety of olives and growing conditions, and to some degree the manner in which the olives are harvested and handled.

- "Olive oil" or "pure olive oil" is the usual name for a more refined and less flavorful olive oil with some virgin olive oil blended in to provide the fruitiness and aroma.

- Since some of the olive oil flavor dissipates under heat, olive oil is acceptable for cooking; extra-virgin is the best choice in uncooked recipes or if added for flavor in the final stages of cooking.

- Oils can turn rancid if stored at room temperature, so keep them in a cool, dark place for up to 6 months; refrigerated they will keep up to 1 year. When chilled, olive oil will temporarily turn partially or totally cloudy and too thick to pour. Just let the oil or dressing come to room temperature or briefly place the closed container under warm running water, and it will be ready to use.

chapter 2

Broiled, Grilled, and Baked Chicken

MARINATING ADDS A WHOLE NEW PALETTE OF WAYS
to flavor chicken and is one of the best ways to add flavor without adding fat. If you're accustomed to using bottled Italian dressing as a quick marinade, read on.

A typical made-from-scratch marinade has three components: acid, oil, and aromatics. The acid (lemon or lime juice, wine, or vinegar) acts as a tenderizer. The oil coats the chicken, preventing it from drying out during cooking. The aromatics add flavor.

To make the most of your marinades, here are a few simple suggestions:

- Use a covered glass, ceramic, stainless steel, or plastic container for marinating. Aluminum and cast iron tend to react with acids and give the dish an off flavor.

- Begin with very fresh chicken and always marinate your chicken in the refrigerator.

- It is not necessary for the chicken to be completely submerged in a liquid marinade, but it should be turned several times while marinating so that the chicken is evenly coated. (A simple method is to place the chicken and a liquid marinade in a zip-seal plastic bag; turn the bag occasionally to coat the chicken.)

- The longer the food is left in a marinade, the more flavor it absorbs. Thirty minutes is the minimum for adequate flavor, 24 hours the maximum to prevent harmful bacteria from growing (see "Chicken Safety," page xiv).

- Be sure to drain the marinated chicken well before broiling or grilling; during cooking, use the reserved marinade for basting with a basting brush, bulb baster, or spoon. Discard the remaining marinade. Do not reuse a marinade or use it as a sauce (cooked or uncooked) for the cooked chicken, because of the possible dangers from bacteria. (Note: The nutritional analyses for dishes with marinades reflect the amount of the marinade that is absorbed by the chicken and do not include the discarded portion.)

- For the best flavor and texture, marinated chicken should be taken from the refrigerator about 15 minutes before broiling or grilling. Chilled chicken requires longer to cook and can have a tougher texture.

Although marinating requires advance thought and planning, the marinated chicken in these recipes can be on the table in just 10 minutes after cooking begins. The recipes use a variety of cooking methods: broiling, barbecuing, stovetop grilling, and baking.

Marinated chicken is ideal for broiling. Position the oven broiler rack 4 to 5 inches from the heating element. Preheat the broiler for at least 5 minutes. Broil the chicken breasts for

5 minutes; turn and brush with the marinade. Continue to broil for about 5 minutes or until the chicken is thoroughly cooked.

To prepare for cooking on an outdoor barbecue, allow a full bed of charcoal briquettes to burn until they become glowing coals covered with a layer of gray ash. Grill the chicken for about 5 minutes per side, basting once with the marinade, until the chicken is thoroughly cooked.

I often prepare my marinated chicken on a nonstick stovetop grill, which is one of my most-used pieces of cookware. Available in a variety of materials and in a range of shapes and sizes, these pans can be found in most cookware departments. I'd say this appliance is a must. Not only does the chicken cook quickly (about 5 minutes per side), but it also acquires a smoky, grilled flavor along with those visually appealing grill lines.

Marinated (and drained) chicken breasts can also be baked, uncovered, at 400°F for about 10 minutes. Using this method, the chicken does not become as brown and crisp as it does when cooked with the direct, intense heat of the grill or broiler. The flavors are delicious; however, the texture will be less desirable for use in warm chicken salads.

Here are a few cooking basics:

- Chicken is done when it is cooked through at the thickest points. When broiling or grilling, always turn the chicken breasts halfway through the cooking period to ensure even and complete cooking. Do the same when the chicken is cubed and cooked on skewers with vegetables. Remember that recipe cooking times are approximate, since the heat of broilers and barbecue grills can vary. If the chicken breast halves vary greatly in size, flatten them to an even thickness before grilling so they will finish cooking at the same time.

- When cooking chicken that's been marinated or basted with a sauce containing tomato, sugar, or honey, it may be necessary to reduce the heat and watch closely to prevent overbrowning or burning as these ingredients caramelize.

- To broil or grill a chicken breast without marinating, pat the chicken dry with paper towels and then brush both sides with oil (olive oil is a good choice since it adds flavor and aroma); sprinkle with dried herbs and pepper before cooking.

- For moist chicken, turn pieces with tongs instead of piercing with a fork. Piercing the skin releases juices and dries out the chicken.

- For even cooking, place meatier pieces in the center and smaller pieces toward the edges of the broiler, barbecue, or stovetop grill.

I have included instructions for my favorite accompaniments and side dishes. A simple green salad, hearty bread, steamed vegetables, and rice or pasta will also make your meal complete. Because the chicken requires so little time to cook, be sure to start your accompaniments before placing your entrée under the broiler or on the grill.

The marinated chicken dishes are meant to be served warm, but many are also delicious chilled. Chilled chicken can be sliced and made into a sandwich served in pita bread pockets, or as a salad ingredient, with the chicken served atop a bed of greens. Some of the Variations suggest dressings to turn your chicken into an out-of-the-ordinary salad. Chicken enhanced with a marinade can elevate even the simplest chicken salad of chicken cubes tossed with celery and mayonnaise from so-so to sublime.

Among the gems in this chapter, you will also find two recipes for grilled chicken with creative sauces: Grilled Chicken with Pesto Sauce (page 86) and Grilled Chicken with Tomato–Sweet Red Pepper Sauce (page 82), both of which have varied uses. The baked Parmesan Chicken (page 84) is reminiscent of crispy fried chicken, but with much less fat and far more flavor.

chicken
with **balsamic**
vinaigrette

Makes 4 servings

Here the Balsamic Vinaigrette serves both as a marinade and as the dressing for the perfect accompaniment, Corn and Rice Salad (page 93). This combination is one of my personal favorites.

Balsamic Vinaigrette

$1/2$ cup balsamic vinegar

$1/4$ cup extra-virgin olive oil

$1/4$ cup water

2 teaspoons Dijon mustard

2 teaspoons light brown sugar

1 teaspoon minced garlic

$1/4$ teaspoon pepper, or to taste

To Complete the Recipe

Olive oil or nonstick cooking spray

4 boneless skinless chicken breast halves
   (about 4 ounces each)

GARNISH (OPTIONAL)   sprigs of fresh basil

1. To prepare the vinaigrette, whisk together all the ingredients in a small bowl or measuring cup until the brown sugar has dissolved. Adjust the seasoning to taste.

2. Pour $1/4$ cup of the vinaigrette into a shallow pan or baking dish. Place the chicken breasts in the vinaigrette; cover with another $1/4$ cup of the vinaigrette. (Reserve the remaining vinaigrette for the Corn and Rice Salad accompaniment or as a salad dressing.)

(continues)

3. Refrigerate, covered, for at least 30 minutes, or for as long as 24 hours, turning the chicken occasionally.

4. When ready to cook, position the oven broiler rack 4 to 5 inches from the heating element; preheat the broiler. Lightly oil a broiler pan or baking sheet. Remove the chicken breasts from the marinade and place them on the prepared pan; reserve the excess marinade.

5. Broil the chicken for 5 minutes; turn and brush with the marinade. Continue to broil for about 5 minutes or until the chicken is thoroughly cooked; discard the remaining marinade.

PER SERVING: Cal 202/Prot 32.9g/Carb 2.4g/Fat 6.8g/Chol 87mg/Sod 74mg

ADVANCE PREPARATION   The Balsamic Vinaigrette will keep for up to 1 week in a tightly closed container in the refrigerator. The Chicken with Balsamic Vinaigrette can be prepared up to 1 day in advance, refrigerated, and served chilled or at room temperature.

Variations

• Serve the cooked chicken (warm or chilled and cut into strips) on a bed of mesclun tossed with the Balsamic Vinaigrette.

• To turn this dish into a meal-sized composed salad, add wedges of plum tomatoes and steamed asparagus spears.

Chicken with Balsamic Vinaigrette served with Corn and Rice Salad

apricot-glazed
chicken

Makes 4 servings

Apricot-Glazed Chicken pairs well with Couscous with Apricots and Cilantro (page 99), which can be prepared either while the chicken marinates or while it cooks. For color and texture, add steamed vegetables such as asparagus, green beans, carrots, or snap peas. Since nearly all fruits are compatible with chicken, feel free to improvise and substitute other fruit jams in the marinade—orange marmalade is especially great. Try it!

Apricot Marinade

$1/4$ cup apricot jam

2 tablespoons red wine vinegar (see Tips)

1 tablespoon canola or safflower oil

2 teaspoons finely minced fresh ginger

$1/4$ teaspoon pepper

To Complete the Recipe

Canola oil, safflower oil, or nonstick
   cooking spray

4 boneless skinless chicken breast halves
   (about 4 ounces each)

GARNISH (OPTIONAL)   sprigs of fresh mint, cilantro, or parsley

1. Stir together the marinade ingredients in a small bowl or measuring cup.

2. Pour half of the marinade into a shallow pan or baking dish. Place the chicken breasts in the marinade; cover with the remaining marinade.

3. Refrigerate, covered, for at least 30 minutes, or for as long as 24 hours, turning the chicken occasionally.

4. When ready to cook, position the oven broiler rack 4 to 5 inches from the heating element; preheat the broiler. Lightly oil a broiler pan or baking sheet (see Tips). Remove the chicken breasts from the marinade and place them on the prepared pan; reserve the excess marinade.

5. Broil the chicken for 5 minutes; turn and brush with the marinade. Continue to broil for about 5 minutes or until the chicken is thoroughly cooked; discard the remaining marinade.

PER SERVING: Cal 207/Prot 32.8g/Carb 7.4g/Fat 5.1g/Chol 87mg/Sod 72mg

ADVANCE PREPARATION   The Apricot-Glazed Chicken can be cooked up to 1 day in advance, refrigerated, and served chilled or at room temperature.

Variations

- For Orange-Glazed Chicken, prepare the marinade by combining 2 tablespoons orange marmalade, 1 tablespoon red wine vinegar, 1/2 teaspoon crushed dried rosemary, and a dash of pepper.

- Serve the cooked chicken (warm or chilled and cut into strips) on a bed of greens tossed with a light dressing such as Sesame-Soy Dressing (page 126), Cilantro Vinaigrette (page 142), Sesame-Ginger dressing (page 124), Ginger-Soy Vinaigrette (page 154), or Sesame-Orange Dressing (page 156).

> ## TIPS
>
> - Wine vinegars are produced from the acetic fermentation of wine; they are mellow in flavor and retain the aroma of the wine from which they are made. The name vinegar comes from the French *vin aigre,* which means "sour wine."
>
> - In place of nonstick cooking spray, use a paper towel to spread oil lightly on a pan or baking sheet. Or line your baking sheet with kitchen parchment, which not only eliminates the need for oil but also provides for simple cleanup.

plum-glazed
chicken

Makes 4 servings

Plum marinade can be prepared with a minimum of ingredients, which you can keep on hand. To complete the Asian theme, serve the broiled or grilled chicken with steamed snow peas and Sesame Rice (page 98).

Plum Marinade

1/4 cup Chinese plum sauce (see Tip)

2 tablespoons white rice vinegar

1 teaspoon Dijon mustard

1 teaspoon minced garlic

1/4 teaspoon red pepper flakes

To Complete the Recipe

Canola or safflower oil or nonstick cooking
   spray

4 boneless skinless chicken breast halves
   (about 4 ounces each)

GARNISH (OPTIONAL)   sprigs of fresh cilantro, mint, or parsley

1. Stir together the marinade ingredients in a small bowl or measuring cup.

2. Pour half of the marinade into a shallow pan or baking dish. Place the chicken breasts in the marinade; cover with the remaining marinade.

3. Refrigerate, covered, for at least 30 minutes, or for as long as 24 hours, turning the chicken occasionally.

4. When ready to cook, position the oven broiler rack 4 to 5 inches from the heating element; preheat the broiler. Lightly oil a broiler pan or baking sheet. Remove the chicken breasts from the marinade and place them on the prepared pan; reserve the excess marinade.

5. Broil the chicken for 5 minutes; turn and brush with the marinade. Continue to broil for about 5 minutes or until the chicken is thoroughly cooked; discard the remaining marinade.

PER SERVING: Cal 176/Prot 32.9g/Carb 3.1g/Fat 3.5g/Chol 87mg/Sod 74mg

ADVANCE PREPARATION   The Plum-Glazed Chicken can be cooked up to 1 day in advance, refrigerated, and served, chilled or at room temperature.

Variation

• Serve the cooked chicken (warm or chilled and cut into strips) on a bed of greens tossed with a light dressing such as Sesame-Soy Dressing (page 126), Cilantro Vinaigrette (page 142), Sesame-Ginger Dressing (page 124), Ginger-Soy Vinaigrette (page 154), or Sesame-Orange Dressing (page 156).

> ## TIP
>
> Chinese plum sauce is a thick, sweet-and-sour sauce made from plums, apricots, chili peppers, sugar, vinegar, and spices. It is usually used as a condiment but also makes a tasty ingredient in sauces. Look for it in the Asian section of most supermarkets. Store in the refrigerator after opening.

citrus
chicken

Makes 4 servings

The fruity flavor in this recipe, and in the Kiwi-Lime Salsa (page 91) or Couscous with Sesame-Orange Dressing (page 100) accompaniment, is a welcome treat during the hot summer months. For variety, serve the chicken chilled on a bed of salad spinach leaves.

Citrus Marinade

2 teaspoons grated orange rind

2 tablespoons fresh orange juice

2 tablespoons fresh lemon juice

2 tablespoons fresh lime juice

2 tablespoons dry sherry

1 tablespoon canola or safflower oil

1 tablespoon minced shallot (see Tip)

1/4 teaspoon pepper

To Complete the Recipe

Canola or safflower oil or nonstick cooking
  spray

4 boneless skinless chicken breast halves
  (about 4 ounces each)

1. Stir together the marinade ingredients in a small bowl or measuring cup.

2. Pour half of the marinade into a shallow pan or baking dish. Place the chicken breasts in the marinade; cover with the remaining marinade.

3. Refrigerate, covered, for at least 30 minutes, or for as long as 24 hours, turning the chicken occasionally.

4. When ready to cook, position the oven broiler rack 4 to 5 inches from the heating element; preheat the broiler. Lightly oil a broiler pan or baking sheet. Remove the chicken breasts from the marinade and place them on the prepared pan; reserve the excess marinade.

5. Broil the chicken for 5 minutes; turn and brush with the marinade. Continue to broil for about 5 minutes or until the chicken is thoroughly cooked; discard the remaining marinade.

PER SERVING: Cal 186/Prot 32.9g/Carb 1.8g/Fat 5.2g/Chol 87mg/Sod 71mg

ADVANCE PREPARATION   The Citrus Chicken can be cooked up to 1 day in advance, refrigerate, and serve chilled or at room temperature.

Variation

- Serve the cooked chicken (warm or chilled and cut into strips) on a bed of greens tossed with a light dressing such as Cilantro Vinaigrette (page 142) or Sesame-Orange Dressing (page 156).

> ## TIP
>
> A member of the onion family, shallots are small, bulbous herbs with a mild onion-garlic flavor. Always use fresh shallots; dehydrated or powdered products will not do. (If unavailable, substitute some fresh onion and fresh garlic.) Fresh shallots will keep for up to 1 month in the bottom bin of your refrigerator; use them before they begin to sprout. When cooking, don't allow them to brown or they will taste bitter.

with # chicken sherry
marinade

Makes 4 servings

Sherry wine provides a flavor far superior to salty "cooking sherry." Here, sherry is the acid that helps to tenderize the chicken as it marinates. Serve with Steamed Vegetables with Sherry-Mustard Sauce (page 94).

Sherry Marinade

2 tablespoons low-sodium soy sauce

1 tablespoon dry sherry (see Tip)

1 tablespoon canola or safflower oil

$1/2$ teaspoon minced garlic

$1/2$ teaspoon finely minced fresh ginger

$1/4$ teaspoon pepper

To Complete the Recipe

Olive oil or nonstick cooking spray

4 boneless skinless chicken breast halves,
    about 4 ounces each

1. Whisk together the marinade ingredients in a small bowl or measuring cup.

2. Pour half of the marinade into a shallow pan or baking dish. Place the chicken breasts in the marinade; cover with remaining marinade.

3. Refrigerate, covered, for at least 30 minutes, or for as long as 24 hours, turning the chicken occasionally.

4. When ready to cook, position the oven broiler rack 4 to 5 inches from the heating element; preheat the broiler. Lightly oil a broiler pan or baking sheet. Remove the chicken breasts from the marinade and place them on the prepared pan; reserve the excess marinade.

5. Broil the chicken for 5 minutes; turn and brush with the marinade. Continue to broil for about 5 minutes or until the chicken is thoroughly cooked; discard the remaining marinade.

PER SERVING: Cal 181/Prot 33.2g/Carb 0.6g/Fat 5.1g/Chol 87mg/Sod 210mg

ADVANCE PREPARATION   The Chicken with Sherry Marinade can be cooked up to 1 day in advance, refrigerated, and served chilled or at room temperature.

> ## TIP
>
> Sherry is a wine to which brandy has been added to increase the flavor and alcohol content. Sherries vary in color, flavor, and sweetness. Finos are dry and light; manzanillas are very dry, delicate finos with a hint of saltiness. Olorosos, often labeled cream or golden sherry, are darker in color and sweet.

tandoori
chicken

Makes 4 servings

This recipe uses an adaptation of a traditional Indian yogurt marinade for chicken. The yogurt, a natural tenderizer, gives the chicken a velvety texture and tempers the heat of the chili powder; it also keeps the chicken from drying out as it broils. Serve Tandoori Chicken with basmati rice and Sweet-and-Sour Cucumber Slices (page 96) for an Indian-style feast.

Tandoori Marinade

1/2 cup low-fat plain yogurt

2 tablespoons fresh lime juice

1 teaspoon finely minced fresh ginger

1 teaspoon chili powder

1/2 teaspoon minced garlic

1/2 teaspoon paprika

1/4 teaspoon ground cinnamon

1/4 teaspoon pepper

1/4 teaspoon ground cumin

To Complete the Recipe

Canola or safflower oil or nonstick cooking spray

4 boneless skinless chicken breast halves (about 4 ounces each)

GARNISH (OPTIONAL)   finely chopped scallions, sprigs of fresh cilantro, parsley, or mint

1. Whisk together the marinade ingredients in a small mixing bowl.

2. Pour half of the marinade into the bottom of a shallow pan or baking dish. Place the chicken breasts in the marinade; cover with the remaining marinade. Refrigerate, covered, for at least 30 minutes, or for as long as 24 hours.

3. When ready to cook, position the oven broiler rack 4 to 5 inches from the heating element; preheat the broiler. Lightly oil a broiler pan or baking sheet. Remove the chicken breasts from the marinade and place them on the prepared pan. Discard the remaining marinade.

4. Broil the chicken for 5 minutes. Turn and continue to broil for about 5 minutes or until the chicken is thoroughly cooked.

PER SERVING: Cal 176/Prot 33.7g/Carb 1.9g/Fat 3.7g/Chol 88mg/Sod 84mg

ADVANCE PREPARATION   The Tandoori Chicken can be cooked up to 1 day in advance, refrigerated, and served within a day, chilled or at room temperature.

Variation

• Slice the cooked chicken into thin strips and stuff into pita bread pockets along with leafy greens; top with a dollop of plain yogurt mixed with a spoonful of mango chutney or Sweet-and-Sour Cucumber Slices.

teriyaki
chicken

Makes 4 servings

This version of teriyaki contains several traditional ingredients but is sweetened with pure maple syrup. I like to accompany the dish with Chinese Wheat-flour Noodles with Sesame-Pepper Dressing (page 102) to complement the Asian flavors.

Teriyaki Marinade

$1/4$ cup mirin (see Tips)	2 teaspoons finely minced fresh ginger
1 tablespoon low-sodium soy sauce	2 teaspoons dark sesame oil
1 tablespoon pure maple syrup (see Tips)	1 teaspoon minced garlic

To Complete the Recipe

Canola or safflower oil or nonstick cooking spray	4 boneless skinless chicken breast halves (about 4 ounces each)

GARNISH (OPTIONAL)   toasted sesame seeds, sprigs of fresh cilantro

1. Stir together the marinade ingredients in a small bowl or measuring cup.

2. Pour half of the marinade into a shallow pan or baking dish. Place the chicken breasts in the marinade; cover with the remaining marinade.

3. Refrigerate, covered, for at least 30 minutes, or for as long as 24 hours, turning the chicken occasionally.

4. When ready to cook, position the oven broiler rack 4 to 5 inches from the heating element; preheat the broiler. Lightly oil a broiler pan or baking sheet. Remove the chicken breasts from the marinade and place them on the prepared pan; reserve the excess marinade.

5. Broil the chicken for 5 minutes; turn and brush with the marinade. Continue to broil for about 5 minutes or until the chicken is thoroughly cooked; discard the remaining marinade.

PER SERVING: Cal 178/Prot 33.1g/Carb 1g/Fat 4.6g/Chol 87mg/Sod 141mg

ADVANCE PREPARATION   The Teriyaki Chicken can be cooked up to 1 day in advance, refrigerated, and served chilled or at room temperature.

Variations

- Cut the chicken breasts into 1-inch pieces; thread onto eight 6-inch bamboo skewers. Broil or grill for 5 minutes, turn, brush with the marinade, and cook for about 5 minutes more or until the chicken is thoroughly cooked.

- Serve the cooked chicken (warm or chilled and cut into strips) on a bed of greens tossed with a dressing, such as Sesame-Orange Dressing (page 156) or Sesame-Soy Dressing (page 126).

TIPS

- Mirin, a sweet rice wine used for cooking, is used as a seasoning and sweetener. During cooking, the alcohol evaporates, leaving a sweet flavor and glaze that is distinctly Japanese. Mirin is available in Asian markets and in the gourmet or Asian section of many supermarkets.

- For the best flavor and quality, buy "pure" maple syrup, not "maple-flavored" syrup, which is stretched with corn syrup. Even less desirable is "pancake syrup," which rarely contains any maple syrup at all. Once opened, maple syrup should be refrigerated. If crystals develop, place the container in a pan of hot water until they disappear.

chicken
satays
with peanut-ginger sauce

Makes 4 entree servings (2 skewers each)

These tasty kabobs with an Indonesian influence make an unusual and enticing entrée. Rice, a steamed vegetable, and Sweet-and-Sour Cucumber Slices (page 96) are pleasing complements to the sweet-hot flavors. I like to make the Peanut-Ginger Sauce in advance, allowing the flavors to develop a day or so. This recipe also makes an appetizer requiring little last-minute attention.

Peanut-Ginger Sauce

1/4 cup smooth peanut butter (see Tips)

2 tablespoons fresh lemon juice

1 tablespoon low-sodium soy sauce

1/2 teaspoon finely minced fresh ginger

1/2 teaspoon minced garlic

1/4 teaspoon red pepper flakes, or to taste

1 tablespoon water, or as needed

Soy-Ginger Marinade

2 tablespoons low-sodium soy sauce

2 tablespoons fresh lemon juice

1 teaspoon finely minced fresh ginger

1 teaspoon honey

To Complete the Recipe

12 ounces boneless skinless chicken
breast halves, cut into 1-inch pieces

Roasted peanut, canola, or safflower oil, or
nonstick cooking spray

8 (6-inch) bamboo skewers (see Tips)

GARNISH (OPTIONAL)   orange slices and sprigs of fresh cilantro

1. In a small bowl, stir together the sauce ingredients. (The sauce should have a cake-batter consistency; add water as needed.) Cover and allow to stand for at least 30 minutes or refrigerate for up to 3 days. Adjust the seasoning to taste.

2. Stir together the marinade ingredients in a medium bowl. Add the chicken and stir to coat evenly. Cover and refrigerate for at least 30 minutes, or for as long as 24 hours, stirring occasionally.

3. When ready to cook, position the oven broiler rack 4 to 5 inches from the heating element; preheat the broiler. Lightly oil a baking sheet or broiler pan. Thread the chicken onto the bamboo skewers; arrange them on the prepared pan. Discard the remaining marinade.

4. Broil the chicken, turning once, for about 6 minutes or until it is lightly charred and cooked through but still moist inside. (Test the center pieces for doneness, since they take the longest to cook.)

5. Serve the warm skewered chicken with the Peanut-Ginger Sauce for dipping.

PER SERVING: Cal 185/Prot 27.7g/Carb 3.7g/Fat 6.6g/Chol 65mg/Sod 438mg

ADVANCE PREPARATION   The Chicken Satays can be cooked up to 1 day in advance, refrigerated, and served chilled or at room temperature. The Peanut-Ginger Sauce will keep for up to 3 days in a tightly closed container in the refrigerator. The sauce will thicken while standing; add water as needed.

> ## TIPS
>
> - Buy natural peanut butter with the oil on top; stir in the oil before using. Many processed peanut butters are hydrogenated to prevent separation and have sugars, salt, and stabilizers added.
>
> - To prevent them from burning and darkening under the broiler, soak bamboo or wooden skewers in water for 30 minutes before threading on the ingredients.

grilled chicken
with tomato–
sweet red pepper sauce

Makes 4 servings

I often serve this dish on a bed of pasta, such as vermicelli. The sauce will keep for a couple of days; it's also delicious without chicken as a sauce for pasta, crepes, or omelets, either as is or puréed.

Tomato–Sweet Red Pepper Sauce

1 tablespoon olive oil

$1/2$ cup diced red bell pepper (see Tip)

2 teaspoons minced garlic

1 ($14^1/2$-ounce) can diced tomatoes, with juice

$1/2$ cup oil-packed sun-dried tomatoes, drained and coarsely chopped

2 tablespoons minced flat-leaf parsley

2 tablespoons minced fresh basil (or 1 teaspoon dried basil)

$1/2$ teaspoon sugar

$1/4$ teaspoon red pepper flakes, or to taste

$1/4$ teaspoon pepper, or to taste

To Complete the Recipe

1 tablespoon olive oil, divided

4 boneless skinless chicken breast halves (about 4 ounces each)

GARNISH (OPTIONAL)   freshly ground black pepper, freshly grated Parmesan cheese, chèvre cheese, sprigs of fresh flat-leaf parsley

1. To prepare the sauce, heat the oil in a medium saucepan over medium-high heat. Add the bell pepper and garlic; cook, stirring occasionally, for about 3 minutes or until the pepper begins to soften. Stir in the remaining sauce ingredients, except for the fresh basil (if using).

2. Reduce the heat to medium-low; cover and cook, stirring occasionally, for about 10 minutes or until the bell pepper and sun-dried tomatoes are tender. Add the fresh basil (if using) during the last few minutes. Adjust the seasonings to taste.

3. While the sauce is cooking, heat a stovetop grill pan over high heat. Brush one side of each chicken breast with about half of the olive oil. Reduce the heat to medium-high and arrange the chicken on the grill, oiled sides down; cook for about 5 minutes. Brush the top surfaces with the remaining oil; turn and continue to cook for about 5 minutes or until the chicken is lightly browned and thoroughly cooked.

4. To serve, place the chicken on plates; top with the warm sauce.

PER SERVING: Cal 338/Prot 37.4g/Carb 25.7g/Fat 9.5g/Chol 87mg/Sod 273mg

ADVANCE PREPARATION   The sauce can be made up to 2 days in advance; refrigerate in a tightly closed container. Just before serving cook the chicken and warm the sauce.

> ### TIP
>
> Bell peppers are most often sold in the mature green stage, fully developed but not ripe. Red bell peppers are vine-ripened green peppers, which are sweeter because they have ripened longer. Bell peppers are also available in gold, orange, and purple, all mildly flavored. When buying bell peppers, look for plump, firm, crisp vegetables with no wrinkling or soft spots. Store them in plastic bags in the refrigerator. Extra bell peppers can be frozen without blanching: Simply chop them and freeze in small containers or zip-top bags. The thawed peppers will be limp but can be used in cooking.

parmesan
chicken

Makes 4 servings

Reminiscent of crispy fried chicken, this version has much less fat and far more flavor. If time permits, prepare a sauce to use as a topping, such as the Roasted Sweet Red Pepper Sauce (page 46), Pesto Sauce (page 86), or Tomato–Sweet Red Pepper Sauce (page 82).

Olive oil or olive oil cooking spray

4 boneless skinless chicken breast halves (about 4 ounces each)

$1/4$ cup low-fat plain yogurt

$1/4$ cup toasted wheat germ (see Tip)

2 tablespoons freshly grated Parmesan cheese

1 teaspoon dried basil

1 teaspoon dried thyme

$1/2$ teaspoon pepper

$1/8$ teaspoon paprika

1. Preheat the oven to 400°F.

2. Lightly oil a baking sheet or shallow pan; set aside.

3. To prepare the chicken, place the chicken breasts between 2 sheets of plastic wrap or in a plastic bag; flatten them to a $1/2$-inch uniform thickness.

4. Pour the yogurt into a small, shallow bowl.

5. Stir together the wheat germ, Parmesan cheese, basil, thyme, pepper, and paprika in a separate small, shallow bowl.

6. Dip each chicken breast into the yogurt, turning to moisten both sides. Lay the chicken in the wheat germ-Parmesan mixture and press gently; turn to coat the other side, again pressing gently. Place on the prepared baking pan.

7. Bake the chicken for 5 minutes; turn and continue to bake for about 4 minutes or until the chicken is crispy and thoroughly cooked.

PER SERVING: Cal 216/Prot 37g/Carb 4.8g/Fat 5.4g/Chol 90mg/Sod 139mg

Variations

- Substitute other ingredients for the yogurt. Try 1 lightly beaten egg, 2 lightly beaten egg whites, $1/4$ cup cholesterol-free egg substitute, or $1/4$ cup buttermilk.

- Substitute 2 teaspoons of packaged Cajun seasoning for the basil, thyme, and paprika); or omit the pepper too and substitute 2 teaspoons Cajun Seasoning Mix (page 47).

> ### TIP
>
> Wheat germ, usually sold in the cereal aisle of the supermarket, is the embryo of the wheat berry. It is rich in vitamins, minerals, and protein. Toasted wheat germ is preferable to raw wheat germ because of its nuttier flavor and slightly crunchy texture. To prevent rancidity, store wheat germ in a tightly closed container in the refrigerator.

chapter **2** *Broiled, Grilled, and Baked Chicken*

85

grilled
chicken
with pesto sauce

Makes 4 servings

With broiled or sliced tomatoes and fresh corn on the cob as accompaniments, this dish is the ultimate in superb summer dining—yet it is exceptionally easy and quick to prepare. If you're cooking for only two and have leftovers (or just for variety), cut the chicken into cubes and toss it with the pesto sauce and corn cut from the cob as a do-ahead chicken salad; serve the next day on a bed of greens garnished with tomato wedges. The pesto sauce also makes an outstanding sauce for a side dish of steamed vegetables.

Pesto Sauce

2 tablespoons Basil Pesto (page 97)

2 tablespoons low-fat plain yogurt

2 tablespoons garlic-infused olive oil
(see Tip)

2 tablespoons white wine vinegar

$1/4$ teaspoon pepper, or to taste

To Complete the Recipe

1 tablespoon olive oil, divided

4 boneless skinless chicken breast halves
(about 4 ounces each)

$1/4$ teaspoon pepper, or to taste

GARNISH (OPTIONAL)   freshly ground black pepper, freshly grated Parmesan cheese, toasted pine nuts, sprigs of fresh basil

1. To prepare the sauce, whisk together the ingredients in a small saucepan. Adjust the seasoning to taste; set aside.

2. Heat a stovetop grill pan over high heat. Brush one side of each chicken breast with about half of the olive oil. Reduce the heat to medium-high and arrange the chicken on the grill, oiled sides down; cook for about 5 minutes. Brush the top surfaces with the remaining oil; turn and continue to cook for about 5 minutes or until the chicken is lightly browned and thoroughly cooked.

3. While the chicken is cooking, warm the pesto sauce over low heat, stirring occasionally, taking care not to boil.

4. When the chicken is done, sprinkle with pepper. Serve topped with the pesto sauce.

PER SERVING: Cal 275/Prot 33.8g/Carb 2.2g/Fat 14.5g/Chol 88mg/Sod 79mg

ADVANCE PREPARATION   The pesto sauce will keep for up to 2 days in a tightly closed container in the refrigerator. If it thickens while standing, stir in milk or water as needed. Just before serving, cook the chicken and gently warm the sauce, taking care not to boil.

> ## TIP
>
> Garlic-infused or garlic-flavored olive oil is available in many supermarkets and gourmet shops; if you prefer, you may substitute extra-virgin olive oil and add minced garlic to taste.

Chicken Kabobs with Tomato-Soy Marinade

chicken
kabobs
with **tomato-soy marinade**

Makes 4 servings

With chicken and vegetables broiled together, these kabobs are nearly a meal in themselves, needing only the addition of a green salad and hearty bread. If time permits, I also prepare rice and Tomato-Corn Salsa (page 92).

Tomato-Soy Marinade

$1/4$ cup low-sodium soy sauce

1 tablespoon honey

1 tablespoon tomato paste (see Tips)

1 teaspoon minced garlic

$1/4$ teaspoon pepper

To Complete the Recipe

Canola or safflower oil or nonstick cooking spray

12 ounces boneless skinless chicken breast halves, cut into 1-inch pieces

1 (8-ounce) can pineapple chunks in their own juice or 24 (1-inch) cubes fresh pineapple (about $1/2$ medium pineapple)

1 small zucchini, cut into twenty-four $1/4$-inch-thick slices

4 (12-inch) metal skewers

1. Whisk together the marinade ingredients in a glass bowl. Add the chicken and stir to coat. Cover and refrigerate for at least 30 minutes, or for as long as 24 hours, stirring occasionally.

(continues)

2.   When ready to cook, position the oven broiler rack 4 to 5 inches from the heating element; preheat the broiler. Lightly oil a baking sheet or broiler pan. Alternately thread the chicken, pineapple, and zucchini onto skewers. Arrange the skewers on the prepared pan; baste the zucchini and pineapple with the marinade. Set aside the remaining marinade.

3.   Broil for 4 minutes; turn and baste with the marinade. Continue to broil for about 2 minutes or until the chicken is thoroughly cooked. (Test the center pieces for doneness, since they take the longest to cook.) Discard the remaining marinade.

PER SERVING: Cal 166/Prot 26g/Carb 9.2g/Fat 2.8g/Chol 65mg/Sod 334mg

TIPS

- Tomato paste is available in tubes, making it ideal for recipes calling for less than a 6-ounce can.

- "Blanching" means to plunge food quickly into simmering water and then immediately into cold water to stop the cooking. Blanching enhances the color and flavors of vegetables, and also loosens the skins of tomatoes, peaches, and nuts (such as almonds), making them easy to peel.

Variations

- For more tender zucchini, blanch before threading onto the skewers (see Tips).

- As you thread the skewers, substitute other fruit or vegetables for all of part of the pineapple or zucchini (up to 2 cups total). Try mandarin orange segments, mushrooms, chunks of green or red bell pepper, onion slices, and/or cherry tomatoes.

- Sprinkle the kabobs with sesame seeds before broiling.

kiwi-lime
salsa

Makes 4 servings

This recipe can be adapted to use your favorite fruits. Try substituting cubed grapefruit, oranges, papaya, strawberries, or any combination for the kiwi.

1 teaspoon lime zest

1 tablespoon fresh lime juice

1 teaspoon Dijon mustard (see Tips)

2 medium-size kiwis, peeled and cut into
  $1/2$-inch cubes (about 1 cup); (see Tips)

2 medium scallions, finely chopped

1 tablespoon currants

Stir together the lime zest, lime juice, and Dijon mustard in a medium bowl. Add the kiwis, scallions, and currants; toss.

PER SERVING: Cal 35/Prot 5g/Carb 7.9g/Fat .2g/Chol 0mg/Sod 5mg

ADVANCE PREPARATION   Kiwi-Lime Salsa can be made a few hours in advance; cover and refrigerate. For the best flavor, bring to room temperature for serving.

TIPS

- Dijon mustard, which originated in Dijon, France, is made from brown mustard seeds, herbs, spices, and white wine, rendering it more flavorful than ordinary yellow mustard.

- Keep ripe kiwis in the refrigerator for up to 3 weeks. Since they do not discolor after being cut, kiwis are a good choice for fruit salads and desserts.

tomato-corn
salsa

Makes 4 servings

Experiment with other herbs to replace the basil in this salsa to create a medley of accents for marinated chicken breasts.

3 plum tomatoes, cut into $1/4$-inch cubes (about $1^1/2$ cups)

$1/2$ cup frozen corn, thawed

1 medium scallion, finely chopped

2 teaspoons minced jalapeño pepper, or to taste

1 tablespoon fresh lemon juice

1 tablespoon coarsely chopped fresh basil (or $1/2$ teaspoon dried basil)

$1/2$ teaspoon minced garlic (see Tip)

$1/4$ teaspoon pepper, or to taste

Stir together all of the ingredients in a small bowl. Cover and chill for at least 30 minutes to allow the flavors to develop. Adjust the seasonings to taste.

PER SERVING: Cal 38/Prot 1.3g/Carb 7.8g/Fat .2g/Chol 0mg/Sod 28mg

ADVANCE PREPARATION   If you begin with the freshest of ingredients, the Tomato-Corn Salsa will keep in the refrigerator for several days.

TIP

Store garlic heads in a cool, dark, well-ventilated place, such as a garlic cellar (a ceramic pot with holes and a lid); or they can be sealed in a plastic bag and refrigerated. Sprouted garlic cloves are fine to use but are less flavorful. An acceptable alternative to fresh garlic is marinated, minced garlic, which is sold in the produce department of most supermarkets. Refrigerate after opening and always use a clean spoon when measuring it from the jar to avoid bacteria growth. Garlic develops a bitter taste if permitted to brown, so add it near the end of the cooking period unless there is an abundance of moisture in the pan.

Variations

• Substitute for the fresh jalapeño pepper. Try 2 teaspoons canned diced green chilies or 2 teaspoons minced, ripe, red jalapeño peppers from a jar.

• Substitute other herbs for the basil. Try thyme, oregano, or flat-leaf parsley.

corn
and rice
salad

Makes 4 servings

Prepare this while the chicken is marinating. The salad will keep up to 2 days in the refrigerator; however, it is at its best when served the day it is prepared.

1$^1/_2$ cups cooked brown rice

1 cup frozen yellow or white shoepeg corn, thawed (see Tip)

2 plum tomatoes, cut into $^1/_2$-inch cubes (about 1 cup)

$^1/_4$ cup coarsely chopped fresh basil

Freshly ground pepper, to taste

$^1/_2$ cup Balsamic Vinaigrette (page 65)

1. Toss together the rice, corn, tomatoes, basil, and pepper in a medium bowl. Add $^1/_4$ cup of the vinaigrette; toss again. Adjust the seasoning to taste.

2. Cover and refrigerate. Drizzle each serving with additional vinaigrette as the plates are assembled. Serve chilled or at room temperature.

> **TIP**
>
> White shoepeg corn, named for its peglike shape, is available frozen; it has smaller kernels and is sweeter than yellow corn.

PER SERVING: Cal 209/Prot 3.5g/Carb 31.6g/Fat 7.6g/Chol 0mg/Sod 15mg

Variation

• Substitute white rice or wild rice or a combination for all or part of the brown rice (1$^1/_2$ cups total rice).

steamed vegetables
with **sherry-mustard**
sauce

Makes 4 servings

The Sherry-Mustard Sauce is excellent on nearly any vegetable.

2 cups broccoli florets

1 cup cauliflower florets (see Tip)

Sherry-Mustard Sauce

$1/4$ cup reduced-fat cholesterol-free
   mayonnaise

1 tablespoon dry sherry

1 tablespoon fresh lemon juice

1 tablespoon Dijon mustard

$1/4$ teaspoon pepper, or to taste

GARNISH (OPTIONAL)   toasted sesame seeds

1. Put the broccoli and cauliflower florets in a medium microwave-proof dish; add about $1/4$ cup water. Cover and microwave on high for about 5 minutes or until the vegetables are crisp-tender. (Or cook the vegetables for about 6 to 8 minutes in a stovetop steamer.)

2. While the vegetables are cooking, stir together the sauce ingredients in a small bowl. Adjust the seasoning to taste.

3. When the vegetables are done, drain well. Spoon onto serving plates drizzle with the sauce.

PER SERVING: Cal 77/Prot 2.9g/Carb 8.9g/Fat 3.3g/Chol 0mg/Sod 33mg

ADVANCE PREPARATION   The Sherry-Mustard Sauce will keep for up to 2 days in a tightly closed container in the refrigerator. Bring to room temperature before drizzling over warm vegetables. The vegetables can be cooked in advance and served later the same day chilled or at room temperature.

Variations

- Substitute other vegetables for the broccoli and cauliflower (up to 3 cups total). Try asparagus spears or carrots.

- Substitute low-fat plain yogurt for the reduced-fat cholesterol-free mayonnaise.

> ## TIP
>
> When you buy cauliflower, pick one that is white, hard, and tightly packed. Store it in the refrigerator in a sealed plastic bag, stem side up, to keep moisture from collecting on top; use within a day or two. Separated cauliflower florets are the best choice when only a small amount is needed.

sweet-and-sour
cucumber
slices

Makes 4 servings

This refreshing, light salad provides a crunchy texture and a cooling element to complement spicy dishes.

$1/4$ cup white rice vinegar

$1/4$ cup sugar

1 medium cucumber, very thinly sliced

1 small shallot, very thinly sliced

1 tablespoon minced hot red chile pepper
  (seeds removed)

GARNISH (OPTIONAL)   finely chopped fresh cilantro

1. Stir together the vinegar and sugar in a small saucepan; bring to a boil over medium-high heat. Cook, stirring occasionally, just until the sugar dissolves. Remove from the heat and allow to cool.

2. Toss together the cucumber, shallot, and pepper in a medium bowl. Add the vinegar-sugar mixture and stir. Refrigerate until chilled.

PER SERVING: Cal 67/Prot .5g/Carb 16g/Fat .1g/Chol 0mg/Sod 7mg

ADVANCE PREPARATION   This salad can be prepared up to 1 day in advance.

Variation

- Add up to $1/4$ cup thinly sliced uncooked carrots or finely chopped green bell pepper.

basil
pesto

Makes ¹/₂ cup

If you're a basil lover (and who isn't?), you'll find plenty of reasons to keep this reduced-fat Basil Pesto on hand in your freezer! In the summer, I grow my own basil and find this is an ideal way to preserve it. In addition to the recipes that call for Basil Pesto, you can simply toss it with cooked pasta or rice to use as an accompaniment for chicken.

2 cups loosely packed fresh basil leaves (fresh is essential!)

¹/₄ cup pine nuts, preferably toasted (see Tips)

1 tablespoon extra-virgin olive oil

1 teaspoon minced garlic

¹/₄ teaspoon pepper

Process all of the ingredients in a food processor bowl or blender until the mixture is a coarse purée, using a rubber scraper to push down the sides occasionally.

1 TABLESPOON: Cal 40/Prot 1g/Carb 1.7g/Fat 3.2g/Chol 0mg/Sod 6mg

ADVANCE PREPARATION   This pesto will keep up to 1 week in a covered container in the refrigerator; pour a thin film of oil on top of the pesto to prevent discoloration. For longer storage, freeze in a foil-lined custard cup, cover tightly, transfer to a freezer bag for up to 2 months.

> **TIPS**
>
> - Pine nuts (also called pignoli nuts, pignolias, or piñons) are the seeds from the cone of certain pine trees. Their natural oil turns rancid very quickly, so they should be refrigerated for no more than 1 month or frozen for up to 3 months.
>
> - The sweet, mild flavor of pine nuts is enhanced by toasting. Toast them in a small, dry skillet over medium heat, stirring constantly and watching carefully; the nuts will brown in 4 to 5 minutes. Or toast them in the oven: Spread a single layer on an ungreased baking sheet, and bake at 375°F for 4 to 5 minutes, stirring frequently. Immediately remove the nuts from the pan as soon as they are browned. I usually toast 1 cup at a time and freeze the nuts until I need them.

sesame
rice

Makes 4 servings

This accompaniment can be kept quite simple, or it can become more substantial with the addition of chopped scallion, minced green or red bell pepper, or other vegetables such as cut asparagus. Sliced or slivered almonds can replace the sesame seeds.

1 tablespoon canola or safflower oil

1 cup sliced mushrooms

1 teaspoon minced garlic

2 cups cooked rice (brown, white, basmati, wild, or a combination)

1/2 cup frozen peas (preferably baby peas)

1 tablespoon toasted sesame seeds

1 tablespoon minced fresh flat-leaf parsley (see Tip)

1 tablespoon low-sodium soy sauce

1/2 teaspoon dark sesame oil

Dash of ground white pepper, or to taste

TIP

To mince parsley finely, be sure to dry it well with a paper towel or dish towel after cleaning it. Wet or damp parsley tends to stick together in clumps as you mince. Minced parsley can be frozen in small freezer containers and spooned out as needed for recipes.

Heat the canola or safflower oil in a large nonstick skillet over medium-high heat. Add the mushrooms and garlic; cook, stirring occasionally, for about 3 minutes or until the mushrooms are tender. Stir in the remaining ingredients. Cook, stirring occasionally, for about 5 minutes or until heated through. Adjust the seasoning to taste.

PER SERVING: Cal 184/Prot 4.8g/Carb 27.5g/Fat 6.1g/Chol 0mg/Sod 163mg

ADVANCE PREPARATION   Sesame Rice can be made up to 1 day in advance; cover and refrigerate. Add about 1/4 cup water when reheating.

couscous
with **apricots**
and **cilantro**

Makes 4 servings

This simple but exceptionally tasty side dish can be served warm, chilled, or at room temperature.

1 cup chicken broth

1 cup couscous

2 teaspoons orange zest

1 teaspoon lemon zest

1 teaspoon lime zest

$1/4$ cup dried apricots cut into
$1/4$-inch dice

$1/4$ cup coarsely chopped fresh cilantro
(do not substitute dried cilantro—if
fresh is unavailable, substitute $1/4$ cup
coarsely chopped fresh basil or 2 teaspoons dried basil)

1. Pour the chicken broth into a small saucepan; bring nearly to a boil over high heat. Remove the pan from the heat; stir in the couscous and zests. Cover the pan tightly and allow to stand for about 5 to 8 minutes or until the liquid is completely absorbed.

2. Fluff the couscous with a fork and stir in the apricots and cilantro.

PER SERVING: Cal 199/Prot 7.4g/Carb 40.8g/Fat .7g/Chol 0mg/Sod 199mg

ADVANCE PREPARATION   Couscous with Apricots and Cilantro will keep for up to 2 days in a covered container in the refrigerator.

couscous
with **sesame-**
orange dressing

Makes 4 servings

Make this dish as the chicken cooks and serve warm; or, if you prefer, prepare it in advance, refrigerate while the chicken marinates, and serve the couscous chilled or at room temperature.

1 cup water

1 cup couscous (see Tip)

1 carrot, cut into $1/4$-inch dice

$1/2$ cup frozen peas (preferably baby peas), thawed

$1/2$ cup Sesame-Orange Dressing (page 156)

1. Bring the water to a boil in a small saucepan over high heat. Remove the pan from the heat; stir in the couscous. Cover the pan tightly and allow to stand for about 5 to 8 minutes or until the water is completely absorbed.

2. Meanwhile, put the diced carrot in a small microwave-proof dish; add about 2 tablespoons water. Cover and cook in the microwave oven on high for about 3 minutes or until tender. Drain well and allow to cool. (Or steam the carrots in a stovetop steamer for about 3 to 5 minutes or until tender.)

3. Fluff the couscous with a fork. Add the cooked carrot and thawed peas; toss. Add the dressing and toss again.

PER SERVING: Cal 259/Prot 7.5g/Carb 45.6g/Fat 5.2g/Chol 0mg/Sod 77mg

ADVANCE PREPARATION   Couscous with Sesame-Orange Dressing can be prepared up to 2 days in advance. Store in a covered container in the refrigerator.

Variation

- Substitute other vegetables for the carrots or peas (up to $1^1/2$ cups total). Try diced red bell pepper, asparagus in $1/2$-inch pieces, or finely chopped broccoli stalks.

TIP

Couscous, sometimes called Moroccan pasta, is a tiny, beadlike pasta made from semolina flour. It is available in both white and whole wheat varieties in most super- markets, usually in the rice aisle. It keeps almost indefinitely in a tightly closed container in a dark, dry place. This quick-cooking pasta is prepared by combining equal amounts of couscous and hot (nearly boiling) liquid. Then simply let it stand in a covered bowl for about 5 to 8 minutes or until the couscous is tender and the liquid completely absorbed. (Couscous will double in volume as it absorbs the liquid.) Before serving, fluff with a fork. Serve as is or drizzle with a little olive oil; or add vegetables such as diced carrots (steamed or raw) or minced parsley. In addition to making a tasty side dish, couscous can substitute for rice when served with stir-fries or salads calling for rice.

chinese
wheat-flour noodles
with **sesame-pepper**
dressing

Makes 4 servings

Serve this spicy noodle side dish warm, chilled, or at room temperature.

4 ounces Chinese wheat-flour noodles (see
  Tips)

Sesame-Pepper Dressing

2 tablespoons low-sodium soy sauce

2 tablespoons white rice vinegar

1 tablespoon dark sesame oil

$1/4$ teaspoon red pepper flakes

$1/8$ teaspoon pepper, or to taste

1. Bring a large saucepan of water to a boil over high heat. Reduce the heat to medium-high, add the noodles, and cook for about 3 minutes, or according to package instructions until noodles are *al dente*.

2. Meanwhile, whisk together the dressing ingredients in a small bowl or measuring cup.

3. When the noodles are done, drain well, and return to the pan. Whisk the dressing, add it to the noodles, and toss. Adjust the seasoning to taste.

PER SERVING: Cal 136/Prot 3.9g/Carb 22.1g/Fat 3.6g/Chol 0mg/Sod 801mg

ADVANCE PREPARATION   The Sesame-Pepper Dressing will keep for up to 1 week in a tightly closed container in the refrigerator. The completed dish can be refrigerated for up to 2 days.

Variation

- Add up to 1¹/₂ cups uncooked vegetables, such as shredded carrots, diced cucumber, or diced red bell pepper.

TIPS

- Asian noodles come in many varieties. They are made from various flours—such as wheat, rice, potato, or buckwheat—or beans or yams. They can be purchased in Asian markets and in many supermarkets in both fresh and dried forms.

- Chinese wheat-flour noodles are made of wheat flour, cornstarch, salt, and sugar, giving them a consistency and flavor that's different from Italian pastas. For packaging, the dried noodles are compacted into blocks. To cook, break off the portion you need, drop it into boiling water, cook for about 3 minutes, and drain. The noodles can be served immediately after draining, or they can be patted dry and sautéed in oil until lightly browned.

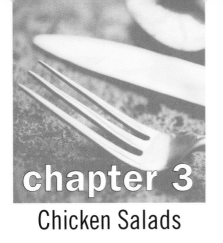

chapter 3

Chicken Salads

"CHICKEN SALAD" MAY BRING TO MIND A TIRED

scenario of cubes of chicken tossed with bits of celery

and smothered in mayonnaise. It's clear that chicken salad

was originally designed as a use for leftovers. But chicken

salad can be much, much more. At its best, it's the star

of a special meal. As we have redefined the salad's role

in dining, it has become difficult to draw the line where

"chicken entrées" end and "chicken salads" begin.

Count on chicken to take your salads beyond the garden variety and turn them into a satisfying and nutritious main course. Or, in smaller portions, chicken salads can share the spotlight with soup and crusty French bread. Take a look at the menus of trendy restaurants: Chicken salads steal the show. Vegetables, fruit, nuts, pasta, and rice beg to be combined with chicken; toss with herbs and a variety of highly flavored dressings, and you will create salads of distinction.

Fortunately for the home cook, supermarket produce departments just get bigger and better. For state-of-the-art salads, we can fill our baskets with fresh produce, thanks to the increased availability of exotic and out-of-season fruits and vegetables from faraway places. And "greens" today include far more than the common iceberg lettuce; mesclun, a gourmet potpourri of young greens, provides a balance of bitter and sweet sensations that add visual, flavor, and texture interest to chicken salads. For speed in preparation, many fruits and vegetables can be purchased already trimmed, and many greens come already cleaned.

In my own menu planning, I think of chicken salads all year long. In the summer, I am inspired by fruit at its juiciest prime; in the winter, I highlight pasta, rice, beans, and winter fruits like pears and grapes. I often select chicken salads as weekend fare for my family and friends, since these creations are ideal for do-ahead one-course meals; and on busy weeknights, it's a treat to sit down to eat something as gorgeous as it is delicious with little mess to clean afterward. When I need a take-along lunch or picnic, I often look to chicken salads for inspiration. Some, such as Mango Chutney Chicken Salad (page 112), can be tossed quickly; They can be prepared early in the day and kept in the refrigerator. For variety, tossed salads such as these can be stuffed into pita bread pockets or rolled in soft tortillas and served as out-of-the-ordinary chicken sandwiches.

Other chicken salads are "composed," with the ingredients arranged with style on individual plates. These visually appealing salads, such as Grilled Chicken and Pear Salad with Hazelnut Vinaigrette (page 140) or Warm Walnut-Chicken Salad (page 148), can become the focal point for more elegant entertaining. Their simplicity demands superior ingredients, including flawless vegetables and fruits at the peak of ripeness and dressings made from top-quality oils and vinegars.

Part of the fun of these salads is contrasting temperatures. Often, I serve warm grilled chicken breasts on cool beds of greens; even in the winter, this makes an appealing entrée. Other times, I serve the same recipe with room-temperature or chilled chicken. Keep in mind that flavors are not at their best when icy-cold; if possible, allow refrigerated salads to stand at room temperature for 10 minutes or so before serving. Do not pour cold salad dressings over warm chicken.

Most often, "stir-fry" brings to mind vegetables—and perhaps chicken—in a sauce, all served atop a bed of warm rice. Not necessarily so! Stir-fried chicken and vegetables can shine as salads, too. A vinaigrette dressing provides delicate Asian flavors, and the mixture is presented on chilled noodles or greens.

Three methods are used for cooking the chicken destined for salads:

- When a grill pan flavor and appearance is most suitable, the chicken breast halves are cooked on a stovetop grill pan or outdoor grill and then cut into strips. Most often, this is the method of choice for warm chicken salads.

- When small pieces of chicken need to be lightly browned, the chicken is sautéed or stir-fried.

- Poaching, or gently simmering food in liquid, is used when a dressing or sauce makes the salad's flavor statement. The poaching liquid for cooking chicken can simply be water; however, since the cooking medium will impart some flavor to the chicken, other possibilities include cooking the chicken in chicken broth, wine, or water seasoned with herbs and spices. Some sources recommend heating the liquid before adding the chicken; others choose to place the chicken in cold liquid and bring the whole thing to a boil. Some say to remove the chicken immediately from the hot liquid; others suggest allowing the chicken to cool in the broth. After experimenting with all of the possibilities, I'm convinced this is the best poaching method for the 15-minute cook:

  1. Pour the liquid into a sauté pan, just large and deep enough to hold the breasts in a single layer. Make certain that the liquid is deep enough to cover the chicken by about $1/2$ inch.

2.   Bring the liquid to a boil over high heat.

3.   Add the chicken and immediately reduce the heat to medium so the water bubbles gently. If cooked too fast, at a full or rolling boil, the meat will become tough.

4.   Cover and simmer until the chicken is just barely past the pink stage; when pierced with a fork, it will be tender and moist inside.

5.   Cooking time will be about 8 to 12 minutes, depending on the thickness of the pieces.

Once the chicken is cooked, it will often be necessary to slice it for your salads. For strips, I use a sharp knife cutting in a sawing motion across the grain of the chicken breasts. To cut chicken into pieces or thin strips, the quickest and easiest method is to use poultry shears.

Dressings give your salads personality. They can be made just before using, but most improve if allowed to stand for about half an hour. When dried herbs are used, this setting time helps to soften their texture and bring out their flavor. Tasted from a spoon, most dressings seem very strong, so it is best to taste by dipping a salad ingredient, such as a leaf of lettuce, into the dressing; then adjust the seasonings, if necessary. Always shake, whisk, or stir dressings before adding them to your salad, because ingredients often separate after sitting. The dressings (some of which are from my book *The Complete Book of Dressings*) can be used on other salads, too. As for greens, wash them well and dry them properly. Water clinging to the leaves will dilute the dressing.

Chicken salads are the perfect medium for improvisation; here's a chance to call on your imagination. Salads can be adapted to whatever is in season as you play with combinations of colors, textures, temperatures, and flavors. Even the fruits, vegetables, beans, and grains from yesterday's meal will perform well in salads today. Add more of your favorite ingredients, and consider the quantities I have listed as mere suggestions. The possibilities are infinite!

red sweet potato salad with chicken

Makes 4 servings

This unusual potato salad with chicken makes a refreshing do-ahead entrée for a hot summer day. For the best flavor—and appearance, too—select yams (or red sweet potatoes) with orange flesh rather than white sweet potatoes.

3 cups yams (red sweet potatoes), peeled and cut into 1-inch cubes (1 large or 2 medium-size yams); (see Tip)

1 tablespoon olive oil

12 ounces boneless skinless chicken breast halves, cut into 1-inch pieces

Dash of pepper, or to taste

2 plum tomatoes, cut into $1/2$-inch cubes (about 1 cup)

2 medium scallions, coarsely chopped

2 tablespoons coarsely chopped fresh basil

$1/2$ cup Balsamic Vinaigrette (page 65)

To Complete the Recipe

4 large leaves leaf lettuce

GARNISH (OPTIONAL)   freshly ground black pepper; and sprigs of fresh flat-leaf basil or parsley

1. Put the yams in a medium microwave-proof dish; add about $1/4$ cup water. Cover and microwave on high (turning the dish halfway through) for about 4 to 5 minutes or until just tender. Drain in a colander and rinse with cool water. (Or cook the yams for about 8 to 10 minutes in a stovetop steamer.)

(continues)

109

2. Meanwhile, heat the oil in a medium skillet over medium-high heat. Add the chicken; cook, stirring occasionally, for about 5 minutes or until it is lightly browned and cooked through. With a slotted spoon, transfer the chicken to a plate; sprinkle it with pepper and set aside to cool.

3. Toss together the yams, chicken, tomatoes, scallions, and basil in a large mixing bowl. Whisk the vinaigrette; add $^1/_4$ cup to the salad and toss again.

4. Transfer the mixture to a large container; cover and chill for at least 1 hour. Serve chilled or at room temperature.

5. To serve, arrange lettuce leaves on serving plates. Top each with a mound of the salad mixture. Whisk the remaining vinaigrette; drizzle about 2 tablespoons over each serving.

PER SERVING: Cal 265/Prot 25.7g/Carb 13.9g/Fat 11.8g/Chol 65mg/Sod 66mg

ADVANCE PREPARATION   This salad will keep for up to 2 days in the refrigerator. Assemble the plates with the additional dressing just before serving.

Variations

- Substitute new potatoes for part of the yams (up to 5 cups total). It is not necessary to peel the new potatoes.

- When tossing the salad, add other ingredients, such as $^1/_4$ cup chopped red or green bell pepper or $^1/_2$ cup steamed cut green beans.

- Serve the salad warm.

TIP

Yams and sweet potatoes are plump, smooth-skinned tubers that are actually not related to potatoes at all. The distinction between yams and sweet potatoes is often confusing, and the names are often interchanged. The flesh of yams (sometimes called red sweet potatoes) is orange and quite sweet when cooked; sweet potatoes (sometimes called white sweet potatoes) have a lighter skin, and the flesh is yellow. Store both in a cool, dark, and dry place for up to 2 weeks; do not refrigerate.

Red Sweet Potato Salad with Chicken

mango
chutney
chicken salad

Makes 4 servings

Accompany this fruity chicken salad with thin wedges of cantaloupe and honeydew melon and whole strawberries—and don't forget the basket of banana muffins.

1 (14^1/$_2$-ounce) can chicken broth
   (2 cups)

Water, as necessary

1 carrot, sliced

^{1}/$_4$ cup sliced onion

2 sprigs of fresh flat-leaf parsley

1 bay leaf

1 pound boneless skinless chicken breast
   halves

Mango Chutney Dressing

3 tablespoons low-fat plain yogurt

2 tablespoons reduced-fat cholesterol-free
   mayonnaise

2 tablespoons mango chutney

1 tablespoon fresh lemon or lime juice

1 teaspoon lemon or lime zest (see Tips)

^{1}/$_4$ teaspoon pepper, or to taste

To Complete the Recipe

^{1}/$_2$ cup halved seedless green or red
   grapes (about 3 ounces)

2 medium scallions, finely chopped

8 leaves romaine lettuce

GARNISH (OPTIONAL) wedges of cantaloupe, strawberries, toasted sliced almonds

1. To poach the chicken breasts, pour the chicken broth into a medium sauté pan; add enough water so that the liquid is about 1½ inches deep. Add the carrot, onion, parsley, and bay leaf. Bring the liquid to a boil over high heat. Add the chicken (it should be covered by about ½ inch liquid); reduce the heat to medium. Cover and cook for about 8 to 10 minutes or until the chicken is just cooked through.

2. With a slotted spoon, remove the chicken from the sauté pan. Cut it into 1-inch pieces, and place on a plate to cool. (Discard the carrot, onion, parsley, bay leaf, and poaching liquid.)

3. Meanwhile, stir together the dressing ingredients in a medium bowl. Adjust the seasoning to taste. Add the grapes, scallions, and chicken; stir until the dressing is evenly distributed.

4. To assemble the servings, line four plates with romaine lettuce leaves. Top each with a mound of chicken salad.

PER SERVING: Cal 226/Prot 34.2g/Carb 10.6g/Fat 5.2g/Chol 88mg/Sod 84mg

ADVANCE PREPARATION   The dressing will keep for up to 2 days in a tightly closed container in the refrigerator. If time permits cover and refrigerate the prepared salad for at least 1 hour or up to 1 day before serving to allow the flavors to develop.

Variation

• Substitute yogurt for the mayonnaise in the mango chutney dressing.

TIPS

• Zesting is done with a kitchen gadget called a zester, which has a short flat blade with a beveled end and 5 small holes. When drawn firmly over the skin of a lemon, lime, or orange, the tool removes long, thin strips of the colored zest. Ideally, prepare zest over the dish you are preparing to make use of the oils, too.

• Before grating or zesting citrus rind, scrub the fruit well, then dry it thoroughly. Remove only the outer, colored part; the white portion beneath tends to taste bitter.

curried
chicken
with **papaya**

Makes 4 servings

I originally developed this recipe for a luncheon that one of my clients served to a group of diet-conscious friends. They loved it, and I think you will, too! For variety, grill the chicken for this recipe.

1 pound boneless skinless chicken breast halves

1 large papaya, peeled, seeded, and cut into 1-inch cubes (about 2 cups)

1 rib celery, coarsely chopped

2 medium scallions, coarsely chopped (see Tip)

1 tablespoon fresh lime juice

Chutney-Yogurt Dressing

$^1/_2$ cup low-fat plain yogurt

2 tablespoons mango chutney

2 teaspoons curry powder, or to taste

$^1/_2$ teaspoon ground cumin

$^1/_4$ teaspoon pepper, or to taste

To Complete the Recipe

4 large leaves leaf lettuce

GARNISH (OPTIONAL)   raw or roasted cashews, dry-roasted unsalted peanuts, or toasted sliced almonds, sprigs of fresh cilantro

1. To poach the chicken breasts, pour water into a medium sauté pan to a level about $1^1/_2$ inches deep. Bring the water to a boil over high heat. Add the chicken (it should be covered by about $^1/_2$ inch water); reduce the heat to medium. Cover and cook for about 8 to 10 minutes until the chicken is just cooked through.

2. With a slotted spoon, remove the chicken from the sauté pan. Cut it into 1-inch pieces, and place on a plate to cool. Discard the poaching liquid.

3. Meanwhile, in a medium bowl, gently toss together the papaya, celery, scallions, and lime juice.

4. Stir together the dressing ingredients in a small bowl or measuring cup. Adjust the seasonings to taste.

5. Add the dressing and chicken to the papaya mixture; toss gently until the dressing is evenly distributed.

6. To serve, place a lettuce leaf on each of 4 salad plates. Top with the chicken salad mixture and garnish.

PER SERVING: Cal 241/Prot 35.2g/Carb 15.7g/Fat 4.2g/Chol 89mg/Sod 105mg

ADVANCE PREPARATION   This salad can be served immediately; but if you prefer to serve it chilled, cover and refrigerate for about 1 hour before serving.

Variation

*   Substitute a mango for the papaya.

> **TIP**
>
> Scallions, also called green onions or spring onions, are delicately flavored members of the onion family. They come from the thinning of immature onion bulbs as well as certain kinds of onions that produce long, thin stems. The leaves should be bright green and firm; the white bottoms should be firm, unblemished, and free of soil. Both parts can be used in recipes calling for scallions. As a rule, the more slender the bottoms, the sweeter the flavor. Store for up to 1 week, wrapped in a plastic bag, in the vegetable crisper section of the refrigerator.

warm
five-spice
chicken salad

Makes 4 servings

*One romantic evening, I savored a shrimp appetizer in a nouvelle Chinese restaurant. It
inspired this scrumptious recipe. The Chinese plum sauce and five-spice powder are the
secrets!*

3 tablespoons roasted peanut oil, divided

12 ounces boneless skinless chicken
breast halves, cut into 2-inch by $1/4$-
inch strips

$1/3$ cup Chinese plum sauce

1 tablespoon water, or as needed

6 cups coarsely shredded romaine leaves

4 ribs bok choy, cut into $1/4$-inch slices;
(also shred green tops); (see Tips)

1 red bell pepper, diced

4 medium scallions, finely chopped

2 teaspoons minced garlic

1 teaspoon Chinese five-spice powder
(see Tips)

Dash of ground white pepper, or to taste

Dash of salt, or to taste

GARNISH (OPTIONAL)   toasted pine nuts or coarsely chopped dry-roasted unsalted peanuts

1. Heat 1 tablespoon of the oil in a large nonstick skillet over medium-high heat. Add
    the chicken; cook, stirring occasionally for about 5 minutes or until it is lightly
    browned and cooked through.

2. With a slotted spoon, transfer the chicken to a bowl and cover to keep warm.

3. Meanwhile, stir together the Chinese plum sauce and the water in a small bowl. (The
    completed sauce should have a maple-syrup consistency; it may be necessary to add
    more or less water.) Set aside.

4. Toss the romaine lettuce with 1 tablespoon peanut oil in a large bowl. Divide among four serving plates; set aside.

5. Heat the remaining 1 tablespoon of oil in the same skillet on medium-high heat. Add the bok choy, bell pepper, and scallions; cook, stirring occasionally, for about 3 minutes or until the bok choy and bell pepper are crisp-tender. Stir in the garlic; cook 30 seconds more.

6. Stir the cooked chicken into the skillet. Add the five-spice powder, white pepper, and salt; stir gently until warm. Adjust the seasonings to taste.

7. To assemble, top each plate of romaine leaves with a mound of the chicken mixture; drizzle with the plum sauce. Serve warm.

PER SERVING: Cal 310/Prot 26g/Carb 22.5g/Fat 12.9g/Chol 65mg/Sod 98mg

ADVANCE PREPARATION   The chicken-vegetable mixture can be made in advance and served chilled or at room temperature later the same day.

Variations

- Add other vegetables, such as up to $1/2$ cup shredded carrot, chopped bamboo shoots, or fresh bean sprouts or up to 1 cup sliced mushrooms; cook with the bok choy and bell pepper.

- Place a serving of cooked Chinese wheat-flour noodles that have been tossed with a little peanut oil over the lettuce; top with chicken-vegetable mixture.

- Stuff the chicken-vegetable mixture (warm, room temperature, or chilled) into pita bread pockets.

chapter 3 *Chicken Salads*

> **TIPS**
>
> - Bok choy should have dark green leaves attached to crisp, lighter green stalks; leaves and stalks are edible cooked or raw. Store bok choy in a plastic bag in the refrigerator for up to 3 days.
>
> - Chinese five-spice powder is a sweet and pungent mixture of fennel seeds, star anise, Szechuan peppercorns, cinnamon, and cloves. A licorice flavor predominates, thanks to the fennel seeds. Some brands also contain ginger and licorice root.

tex-mex
chicken salad
with **southwestern vinaigrette**

Makes 4 servings

As an accompaniment to this salad, it's hard to beat warmed flour tortillas.

2 teaspoons olive oil

1 tablespoon fresh lemon juice

8 ounces boneless skinless chicken breast halves

Dash of pepper, or to taste

1 (15-ounce) can black beans, drained and rinsed

1 cup frozen corn, thawed

1 large tomato, cut into $1/2$-inch cubes

$1/2$ red bell pepper, coarsely chopped

1 (4-ounce) can diced green chilies, drained

2 medium scallions, coarsely chopped

$1/4$ cup coarsely chopped fresh cilantro (do not substitute dried cilantro; if fresh is unavailable, substitute fresh basil)

Southwestern Vinaigrette

3 tablespoons canola or safflower oil

3 tablespoons red wine vinegar

2 tablespoons fresh lemon juice

$1/2$ teaspoon Dijon mustard

1/2 teaspoon sugar

1/8 teaspoon pepper, or to taste

Pinch of ground cumin, or to taste (see Tips)

To Complete the Recipe

4 cups mixed greens or mesclun (see Tips)

GARNISH (OPTIONAL)   sprigs of fresh cilantro

118

1. Stir together the olive oil and lemon juice in a small bowl.

2. Heat a stovetop grill pan over high heat. Brush one side of each chicken breast with about half of the olive oil–lemon juice mixture. Reduce the heat to medium-high and arrange the chicken on the grill, oiled sides down; cook for about 5 minutes. Brush the tops with the remaining olive oil–lemon juice mixture; turn and continue to cook for about 5 minutes or until the chicken is lightly browned and cooked through. Transfer the chicken to a plate and sprinkle with pepper. Cut the chicken into 1-inch pieces and allow to cool.

3. Meanwhile, toss together the black beans, corn, tomato, bell pepper, green chilies, scallions, and cilantro in a large salad bowl.

4. Whisk together the vinaigrette ingredients in a small bowl or measuring cup. Adjust the seasonings to taste. Add the vinaigrette to the bean-corn mixture and toss lightly. Add the chicken; toss again. For each salad, mound some of the chicken salad mixture on a bed of greens.

PER SERVING: Cal 357/Prot 24.8g/Carb 30.5g/Fat 15.1g/Chol 44mg/Sod 464mg

ADVANCE PREPARATION Southwestern Vinaigrette will keep for up to 2 days in the refrigerator. This salad can be made early the day it is to be served. Prepare with only half of the dressing; add the remainder before serving.

Variation

• Substitute other beans for black beans (up to 1^2/$_3$ cups total). Try garbanzos or cannellini beans.

> ## TIPS
>
> • Mesclun is a salad mix found in specialty produce markets and supermarkets. It is a mixture of young, tender salad greens, including arugula, frisee, mizuma, oak leaf, radicchio, and sorrell. Wash and pat dry before using.
>
> • Cumin is the dried fruit of a plant in the parsley family. Available in both seed and ground forms, it provides an aromatic, nutty, and peppery flavor, which is widely used in Mexican and Indian cooking. It is an essential ingredient in curry and chili powder. It should be stored in a cool, dark place, where it will keep for up to 6 months.

chapter 3 Chicken Salads

pesto
vegetable salad
with chicken

Makes 4 servings

This colorful vegetable and chicken combination makes an elegant light entrée—equally good warm or chilled.

4 cups asparagus in 2-inch-long pieces

2 teaspoons olive oil

12 ounces boneless skinless chicken
    breast halves, cut into 1-inch pieces

Creamy Pesto Dressing

2 tablespoons Basil Pesto (page 97)

2 tablespoons low-fat plain yogurt

2 tablespoons red wine vinegar

1/4 teaspoon pepper, or to taste

To Complete the Recipe

8 leaves leaf lettuce

1/2 red bell pepper, finely chopped

GARNISH (OPTIONAL)   freshly ground black pepper, freshly grated Parmesan cheese

1. Put the asparagus in a large microwave-proof dish; add about 1/4 cup water. Cover and microwave on high for about 5 minutes or until the asparagus is crisp-tender. Drain well; cover to keep warm. (Or cook the asparagus for about 5 to 7 minutes in a stove-top steamer.)

2. Meanwhile, heat the oil in a small skillet over medium-high heat. Add the chicken; cook, stirring occasionally, for about 5 minutes until it is lightly browned and cooked through. Remove from the heat and set aside; cover to keep warm.

3. Stir together the dressing ingredients in a small mixing bowl or measuring cup. Adjust the seasoning to taste.

4. Place a bed of lettuce on four salad plates.

5. Toss together the asparagus, chicken, and bell pepper in a large bowl. Add the dressing; toss again. Mound the warm salad on the lettuce.

PER SERVING: Cal 228/Prot 30.7g/Carb 11.4g/Fat 6.6g/Chol 66mg/Sod 70mg

ADVANCE PREPARATION   The Creamy Pesto Dressing will keep for up to 2 days in a tightly closed container in the refrigerator. If it thickens, stir in milk or water as needed. The prepared salad can be covered and refrigerated for up to 1 day. Serve chilled or at room temperature.

Variations

- Substitute other vegetables for the asparagus (up to 4 cups total). Try shredded carrots or sautéed, julienned carrot strips, finely chopped scallions, tomato cubes, or steamed cut green beans. Toss with the salad.

- Make Pesto Potato Salad with Chicken by substituting about 5 new potatoes (see Tip) for the asparagus, steamed or boiled and cut into 3/4-inch cubes (or use part asparagus and part potatoes).

> **TIP**
>
> New potatoes are young potatoes that are harvested before maturity. They are small, thin-skinned, low in starch, and sweet in flavor. They cook rapidly, compared to mature potatoes; they are good boiled or steamed but are not recommended for mashing. New potatoes are preferable for potato salads because mature baking potatoes break apart too easily and absorb too much of the dressing. New potatoes should be stored at room temperature in a dark place, where they will remain at their best for 1 to 2 weeks. Do not store potatoes in the refrigerator, because the cold will cause their starch to convert to sugar, and they will become sweet and darken when cooked.

gazpacho salad
with grilled
chicken

Makes 4 servings

Dressed with a nonfat vinaigrette, this light entrée can be served as a salad or as the filler for pita bread pockets.

2 teaspoons olive oil, divided

12 ounces boneless skinless chicken breasts

Dash of pepper, or to taste

4 cups torn stemmed salad spinach leaves

3 plum tomatoes, cut into 1/2-inch cubes (about 1 1/2 cups)

1 medium cucumber, chopped (about 1 1/2 cups)

1/2 green bell pepper, coarsely chopped

1 rib celery, coarsely chopped

2 medium scallions, coarsely chopped

Red Wine Vinaigrette

1/4 cup red wine vinegar

2 tablespoons fresh lemon juice

2 tablespoons extra-virgin olive oil

1 tablespoon tomato paste

1 teaspoon minced garlic

1/4 teaspoon hot pepper sauce, or to taste

1/4 teaspoon pepper, or to taste

GARNISH (OPTIONAL)   freshly ground black pepper

1. Heat a stovetop grill pan over high heat. Brush one side of each chicken breast with about half of the oil. Reduce the heat to medium-high and arrange the chicken on the grill, oiled sides down; cook for about 5 minutes. Brush the top surfaces with the remaining oil; turn and continue to cook for about 5 minutes or until the chicken is lightly browned and cooked through.

2. Transfer the chicken to a plate, and sprinkle with pepper. Refrigerate to cool.

3. Meanwhile, spread a layer of the spinach on four salad plates.

4. Toss together the tomatoes, cucumber, bell pepper, celery, and scallions in a medium bowl.

5. Whisk together the vinaigrette ingredients in a small bowl or measuring cup. Adjust the seasonings to taste.

6. Add $1/4$ cup of the vinaigrette to the tomato-cucumber mixture; toss.

7. Mound the gazpacho salad on the spinach. Diagonally slice the chilled (or room temperature) grilled chicken into $1/2$-inch-wide strips; arrange them on top of each salad. Whisk the remaining vinaigrette; drizzle over the salads.

> **TIP**
>
> To toast tortillas, lightly brush both sides with olive oil. Prick the surface of the tortillas in several places with a fork. Place the tortillas directly on an oven rack positioned 4 to 5 inches from a preheated broiling element. Broil for about 1 to 2 minutes on each side or until lightly browned and crispy. Watch closely!

PER SERVING: Cal 246/Prot 27.3g/Carb 9.6g/Fat 10.9g/Chol 65mg/Sod 115mg

ADVANCE PREPARATION   The Red Wine Vinaigrette will keep for up to 2 days in a tightly closed container in the refrigerator. The chicken can be grilled earlier in the day, covered, and refrigerated. Assemble the salads with the dressing just before serving.

Variations

• Add up to $1/2$ cup cooked beans, such as black beans or kidney beans, to the salad mixture.

• Serve the gazpacho salad on a toasted tortilla (see Tip).

chinese
chicken salad
with sesame-ginger dressing

Makes 4 servings

This dish is the star of many a restaurant menu. But it is supremely quick and easy to prepare in the home kitchen, too. To make the servings more substantial, add a layer of Chinese egg noodles or fine egg noodles atop the greens when assembling the salad plates. If you wish, substitute other greens, vegetables, or fruits.

Sesame-Ginger Dressing

2/3 cup white rice vinegar

2 tablespoons low-sodium soy sauce

2 teaspoons dark sesame oil (see Tips)

2 teaspoons finely minced fresh ginger

2 teaspoons sugar

1 teaspoon minced garlic

1 teaspoon toasted sesame seeds

Dash of ground white pepper, or to taste

To Complete the Recipe

1 tablespoon canola or safflower oil, divided

1 pound boneless skinless chicken breast halves

Dash of pepper, or to taste

24 stemmed snow peas

6 cups shredded Chinese cabbage (see Tips)

4 ribs bok choy, coarsely chopped (also shred green tops)

3 medium scallions, coarsely chopped

1 (8-ounce) can mandarin orange segments, drained

GARNISH (OPTIONAL) toasted pine nuts, toasted sesame seeds, toasted sliced or slivered almonds, raisins or currants

1. Bring a medium saucepan of water to a boil over high heat.

2. While the water is coming to a boil, whisk together the dressing ingredients in a small bowl until the sugar is dissolved. Adjust the seasoning to taste. Set aside.

3. Heat a stovetop grill pan over high heat. Brush one side of each chicken breast with about half of the oil. Reduce the heat to medium-high and arrange the chicken on the grill, oiled sides down; cook for about 5 minutes. Brush the top surfaces with the remaining oil; turn and continue to cook for about 5 minutes or until the chicken is lightly browned and thoroughly cooked.

4. Transfer the chicken to a plate, sprinkle with pepper, and cover to keep warm. (If you prefer to serve the salad cold, refrigerate the chicken.)

5. Meanwhile, put the snow peas in a wire mesh strainer; blanch by immersing the strainer and the peas for about 30 seconds in the boiling water. Rinse with cold running water; drain well.

6. Toss together the snow peas, Chinese cabbage, bok choy, and scallions in a large bowl. Whisk the dressing; add $1/2$ cup to the salad mixture and toss again.

7. Spread the salad mixture on four individual serving plates. Slice the chicken into 2-inch-long by $1/2$-inch-wide strips; arrange atop the salad and surround with the mandarin orange segments. Whisk the remaining dressing; drizzle over the salads.

PER SERVING: Cal 299/Prot 37g/Carb 18.5g/Fat 8.6g/Chol 87mg/Sod 364mg

ADVANCE PREPARATION   The Sesame-Ginger Dressing will keep for up to 2 weeks in a tightly closed container in the refrigerator. The salad can be made early on the day it is to be served; cover and refrigerate. Add the dressing to the salad just before serving.

TIPS

- Buy dark, amber-colored sesame oil made from toasted sesame seeds rather than light-colored sesame oils. The light oils are extracted from raw sesame seeds and lack the distinctive strong flavor. Because dark sesame oil is so volatile, it is used as a flavoring rather than a cooking oil, and is added as one of the last steps in a recipe.

- Chinese cabbage, sometimes called napa cabbage or celery cabbage, can be recognized by its solid, oblong heads of long, smooth stalks with crinkly, thick-veined, pale green leaves. Unlike the strong flavor of head cabbage, Chinese cabbage is delicately mild; it can be used raw or in stir-fries. In most supermarkets, it is available year-round. Refrigerate, tightly wrapped, for up to 3 days.

chicken-cucumber
salad
with sesame-soy dressing

Makes 4 servings

This crisp and refreshing salad can be prepared in advance, if you wish. Accompanied by fruit muffins and iced tea, it's an irresistible choice for a steamy summer night.

1 pound boneless skinless chicken breast
   halves

Dash of salt

1 large cucumber, cut into $1/2$-inch cubes
   (about 2 cups); (see Tip)

1 cup coarsely shredded carrots

2 medium scallions, coarsely chopped

Sesame-Soy Dressing

$1/4$ cup low-sodium soy sauce

2 tablespoons dark sesame oil

2 tablespoons rice wine vinegar

2 teaspoons minced garlic

1 teaspoon sugar

To Complete the Recipe

4 large leaves leaf lettuce

GARNISH (OPTIONAL)   toasted sesame seeds

1. To poach the chicken breasts, pour water into a medium sauté pan to a level about $1^1/2$ inches deep. Bring the water to a boil over high heat. Add the salt, then the chicken (it should be covered by about $1/2$ inch water); reduce the heat to medium. Cover and cook for about 8 to 10 minutes or until the chicken is just cooked through.

2. With a slotted spoon, remove the chicken from the sauté pan. Cut it into 2-inch pieces, and place on a plate to cool. Discard the poaching liquid.

3. Meanwhile, toss together the cucumber, carrots, and scallions in a medium bowl.

4. Whisk together the dressing ingredients in a small bowl or measuring cup until the sugar is dissolved.

5. Add the dressing to the cucumber-carrot mixture and toss lightly. Add the chicken; toss again.

6. Arrange a bed of lettuce on four salad plates, and top with the chicken salad.

PER SERVING: Cal 266/Prot 35.1g/Carb 7.9g/Fat 10.4g/Chol 87mg/Sod 610mg

ADVANCE PREPARATION   The Sesame-Soy Dressing will keep for up to 1 week in a tightly closed container in the refrigerator. The salad ingredients can be prepared early on the day it is to be served; add the dressing to the salad just before serving.

Variation

• Substitute other vegetables (up to 3 cups total). Try red bell pepper, celery, jícama, or steamed asparagus tips.

TIP

Many cucumbers are sold with a waxy coating to prolong their shelf life; unfortunately, the wax also seals in pesticides. The only way to remove the wax is by peeling. Better yet, buy unwaxed cucumbers. The elongated European cucumbers (sometimes called hothouse or English cucumbers) are usually the best choice. They are grown hydroponically (in water) without pesticides. They have an excellent mild flavor, a more tender texture, and fewer seeds. Store whole cucumbers, unwashed, in a plastic bag in the refrigerator for up to 10 days; once cut, refrigerate them, tightly wrapped, for up to 5 days.

chicken–cannellini
bean salad
with basil-sherry vinaigrette

Makes 4 servings

Basil-Sherry Vinaigrette adds elegance to a hearty dish of beans and chicken; served warm, this winter salad is a meal on its own; simply add French bread.

2 teaspoons olive oil

12 ounces boneless skinless chicken breast halves, cut into 2-inch-long by $1/2$-inch-wide strips

$1/2$ red bell pepper, cut into 2-inch-long by $1/4$-inch-wide strips

$1/2$ green bell pepper, cut into 2-inch-long by $1/4$-inch-wide strips

1 (19-ounce) can cannellini beans, drained and rinsed (see Tips)

1 cup frozen corn, thawed

$1/4$ cup chopped fresh flat-leaf parsley

Basil-Sherry Vinaigrette

$1/4$ cup fresh lemon juice

2 tablespoons dry sherry

2 tablespoons extra-virgin olive oil

1 tablespoon minced shallot

2 tablespoons coarsely chopped fresh basil (do not substitute dried; if fresh is unavailable, substitute fresh flat-leaf parsley)

$1/4$ teaspoon pepper, or to taste

To Complete the Recipe

12 leaves Boston lettuce

GARNISH (OPTIONAL)   freshly ground black pepper, sprigs of fresh basil or flat-leaf parsley

1. Heat the oil in a large nonstick sauté pan over medium-high heat. Add the chicken; cook, stirring occasionally for about 2 minutes or until it is lightly browned but not cooked through. Add the bell peppers; continue to cook, stirring occasionally, for about 3 minutes or until the vegetables are crisp-tender and the chicken is cooked through.

2. Meanwhile, whisk together the vinaigrette ingredients in a small bowl. Adjust the seasoning to taste.

3. Reduce the heat to medium. Add the beans and corn to the sauté pan; stir gently until just warm. Stir in the parsley and the vinaigrette. (Take care not to evaporate the vinaigrette.)

4. Arrange lettuce on four serving plates; top with a mound of the salad mixture.

PER SERVING: Cal 379/Prot 33.6g/Carb 31.1g/Fat 13.3g/Chol 65mg/Sod 62mg

> **TIPS**
>
> - Cannellini beans are large, white Italian kidney beans. In most supermarkets, they can be found either with the canned beans or with the Italian products.
>
> - Canned beans are an acceptable alternative to cooking them from scratch. Drain and rinse the canned beans before using.

ADVANCE PREPARATION   The vinaigrette will keep for up to 4 days in a tightly closed container in the refrigerator. To serve either chilled or at room temperature, the salad should be made the day it is to be served. Add the dressing to the salad just before serving.

Variation

- Substitute other beans for the cannellini beans. Try red kidney beans or black beans.

chicken
caesar
salad

Makes 4 servings

Hail Caesar, the country's most popular salad. And with the addition of chicken, a good thing just got better. (For food safety, the traditional raw egg has been eliminated from the dressing.) Serve this in large shallow salad bowls.

2 teaspoons olive oil, divided

12 ounces boneless skinless chicken breast halves

Dash of pepper, or to taste

Lemon-Caesar Dressing

$1/3$ cup fresh lemon juice

$1/3$ cup reduced-fat cholesterol-free mayonnaise

2 teaspoons Dijon mustard

1 teaspoon anchovy paste (see Tips)

2 tablespoons minced fresh flat-leaf parsley

1 tablespoon freshly grated Parmesan cheese

$1/2$ teaspoon minced garlic, or to taste

$1/8$ teaspoon pepper, or to taste

Few drops of hot pepper sauce, or to taste

To Complete the Recipe

8 cups romaine lettuce torn into 2-inch pieces (1 medium head); (see Tips)

GARNISH (OPTIONAL)   freshly ground black pepper, freshly grated Parmesan cheese, Herbed Croutons (page 132)

1. Heat a stovetop grill pan over high heat. Brush one side of each chicken breast with about half of the oil. Reduce the heat to medium-high and arrange the chicken on the grill, oiled sides down; cook for about 5 minutes. Brush the top surfaces with the remaining oil; turn and continue to cook for about 5 minutes or until the chicken is lightly browned and thoroughly cooked.

2. Transfer the chicken to a plate and sprinkle with pepper. Cut it into 2-inch-long by 1/2-inch-wide strips and allow to cool.

3. Meanwhile, prepare the dressing: Whisk together the lemon juice, mayonnaise, mustard, and anchovy paste in a small bowl. Stir in the remaining ingredients. Adjust the seasonings to taste.

4. Toss the lettuce with the chicken in a large salad bowl. Add the dressing and toss again.

PER SERVING: Cal 223/Prot 27.8g/Carb 8.7g/Fat 8.6g/Chol 68mg/Sod 164mg

> ## TIPS
>
> - Do not soak lettuce in water. Rinse under cool water and drain completely or blot with a paper towel to remove any excess moisture, or use a salad spinner to remove water from the leaves.
>
> - Anchovy paste comes in a tube like toothpaste and is sold in the canned seafood section of the supermarket. Refrigerate it after opening.

ADVANCE PREPARATION   The Lemon-Caesar Dressing will keep for up to 2 days in a tightly closed container in the refrigerator. The chicken can be cooked and refrigerated early on the day it is to be served. Toss the salad and add the dressing just before serving.

Variation

- Substitute low-fat plain yogurt for the mayonnaise in the Lemon-Caesar Dressing (per serving, this reduces calories to 194 and fat to 6 grams).

herbed
croutons

Makes 4 servings

Croutons are the "little extras" that can transform a simple salad into a crunchy, full-flavored plate.

1 teaspoon olive oil

$1/2$ teaspoon minced garlic

$1/4$ teaspoon dried basil

$1/4$ teaspoon dried oregano

2 slices whole wheat bread, cut into $1/2$-inch squares (see Tip)

TIP

Buy true whole wheat bread by selecting one that contains mostly 100 percent whole wheat, stoneground whole wheat, whole-grain, multigrain, or cracked-wheat flour. Some dark breads are made from white flour with caramel coloring added.

---

1. Heat the oil in a small nonstick skillet over medium heat. Add the garlic, basil, and oregano. Cook, stirring, for about 30 seconds or until herbs are softened and moist.

2. Add the bread cubes; stir for about 3 or minutes or until they are lightly browned and crisp. Transfer the croutons to a plate and set aside to cool. (They will become crisper as they cool.)

PER SERVING: Cal 44/Prot 1.3g/Carb 5.9g/Fat 1.7g/Chol 0mg/Sod 80mg

ADVANCE PREPARATION   The croutons can be made 1 or 2 days in advance. Store in a tin at room temperature. To recrisp, put the croutons on a baking sheet and heat for about 5 minutes at 350°F.

Variation

- Instead of basil and oregano, use thyme, chili powder, or curry powder.

pesto
chicken salad
with **red grapes**

Makes 4 servings

*Sweet and juicy grapes are a zesty "extra" that can revive weary taste buds on a hot
summer night.*

Dash of salt	1 cup coarsely shredded carrots
6 ounces penne rigate (about 2 cups)	1 cup seedless red grapes (about 6 ounces)
12 ounces boneless skinless chicken breast halves	2 medium scallions, coarsely chopped
1/2 cup Creamy Pesto Dressing (page 120)	12 leaves red leaf lettuce

GARNISH (OPTIONAL)   freshly ground black pepper, freshly grated Parmesan cheese, sprigs of
fresh basil

1. Bring a medium pot of water to a boil over high heat; add salt, then the penne (see
    Tip). When the water returns to a boil, stir occasionally to separate the penne. Reduce
    the heat to medium-high and cook for about 10 to 12 minutes, or according to
    package instructions, until noodles are *al dente*. Drain well, rinse with cool water, and
    drain again.

2. While the pasta is cooking, poach the chicken. Pour water into a medium sauté pan
    to a level about 1 1/2 inches deep. Stir in the salt. Bring the water to a boil over high
    heat. Add the chicken (it should be covered by about 1/2 inch water), and reduce the
    heat to medium. Cover and cook for about 8 to 10 minutes or until the chicken is just
    cooked through.

(continues)

3. With a slotted spoon, remove the chicken from the sauté pan. Cut it into 1-inch pieces, and place on a plate to cool. Discard the poaching liquid.

4. Whisk together the dressing ingredients in a small bowl or measuring cup. Adjust the seasoning to taste.

5. Toss together the pasta, chicken, carrots, grapes, and scallions in a medium bowl. Add the dressing; toss again.

6. To serve, arrange lettuce on four salad plates or in shallow bowls. Top with mounds of the chicken salad.

PER SERVING: Cal 237/Prot 28.3g/Carb 18.9g/Fat 5.3g/Chol 80mg/Sod 71mg

ADVANCE PREPARATION   This salad can be made early on the day it is to be served; refrigerate and serve chilled or at room temperature.

Variation

• Substitute other pasta shapes for the penne. Try rotini or rotelli.

TIP

When cooking pasta, be sure to use a large pot that is deeper than it is wide; this allows the pasta to move freely as it cooks and prevents sticking. Keep the heat high so the water does not stop boiling when you add the salt to the pasta. Stir the pasta, reduce the heat to medium-high, and begin timing, being certain to keep the water at a rapid boil throughout the cooking period. Cooking time will depend on the shape and thickness of the pasta. Perfectly cooked pasta should be *al dente*—firm but not hard, and evenly cooked so it offers some resistance to the teeth, yet is cooked through. Drain the pasta as soon as it is done; there is no need to rinse pasta unless you must cool it quickly for use in a chilled pasta salad.

Pesto Chicken Salad with Red Grapes

chicken and rice salad
with **chutney**
vinaigrette

Makes 4 servings

Here is a classic chicken and rice salad, but there's no shadow of the "same old, same old" when it's tossed with a provocative chutney vinaigrette. For the best flavor, do not serve this salad directly from the refrigerator; instead, allow it to stand at room temperature for about 10 to 15 minutes before serving.

2 teaspoons canola safflower oil, divided

8 ounces boneless skinless chicken
  breasts

Chutney Vinaigrette

$1/4$ cup mango chutney

2 tablespoons canola or safflower oil

2 tablespoons white rice vinegar

$1/2$ teaspoon curry powder, or to taste

To Complete the Recipe

2 cups cooked rice (long-grain white or
  brown), at room temperature or chilled
  (see Tips)

1 cup frozen corn, thawed

2 plum tomatoes, cut into $1/2$-inch cubes
  (about 1 cup)

$1/4$ cup coarsely chopped fresh cilantro (do
  not substitute dried cilantro)

$1/2$ teaspoon pepper, or to taste

4 cups shredded stemmed salad spinach
  leaves

GARNISH (OPTIONAL)   toasted sliced almonds

1. Heat a stovetop grill pan over high heat. Brush one side of each chicken breast with about half of the oil. Reduce the heat to medium-high and arrange the chicken on the grill, oiled sides down; cook for about 5 minutes. Brush the top surfaces with the remaining oil; turn and continue to cook for about 5 minutes or until the chicken is lightly browned and thoroughly cooked.

2. Transfer the chicken to a plate; cut it into 1-inch squares and allow to cool.

3. Meanwhile, process all of the vinaigrette ingredients in a blender until smooth. Adjust the seasoning to taste.

4. Toss together the chicken, rice, corn, tomatoes, cilantro, and pepper in a medium bowl.

5. Whisk or stir the vinaigrette; add to the salad and toss. Adjust the seasoning to taste.

6. Serve on beds of spinach.

PER SERVING: Cal 388/Prot 22.4g/Carb 51.2g/Fat 10.4g/Chol 44mg/Sod 92mg

ADVANCE PREPARATION   The vinaigrette will keep up to 4 days in a tightly closed container in the refrigerator. The completed salad will keep for 1 day in the refrigerator. Because the rice absorbs the dressing, add half of the dressing when tossing the salad and drizzle with the remaining vinaigrette just before serving.

Variations

-   Substitute other rice for all or part of the white or brown rice. Try basmati rice, wild rice, or a combination (2 cups total), or cooked orzo.

-   Substitute 1/2 cup Balsamic Vinaigrette (page 65) for the Chutney Vinaigrette; add chopped fresh basil in place of the cilantro and serve on romaine lettuce leaves; for variety, add toasted pine nuts.

> **TIPS**
>
> -   The shelf life of white rice is 1 year or longer when kept in a container with a tight-fitting lid in a dark, dry place. Brown rice will keep for several months if stored in the refrigerator.
>
> -   One cup of raw rice yields 2½ to 3 cups cooked rice.

wild rice–chicken salad
with lime-dill
vinaigrette

Makes 4 servings

The leftovers of this lively mix serve as a simple lunch a day or two later when I'm on the run and have no time for cooking.

1 tablespoon olive oil, divided

1 pound boneless skinless chicken breast halves

Dash of pepper, or to taste

2 cups cooked wild rice

1 cup coarsely shredded carrot

1/2 cup diced cucumber

1/2 cup diced red bell pepper

2 medium scallions, finely chopped

1 tablespoon minced fresh flat-leaf parsley

12 leaves soft greens, such as Boston lettuce

Lime-Dill Vinaigrette

1/4 cup white rice vinegar

1/4 cup fresh lime juice

2 tablespoons extra-virgin olive oil

1 tablespoon snipped fresh dill (or 1 teaspoon dried dill); (see Tip)

1/2 teaspoon pepper, or to taste

1/4 teaspoon sugar

GARNISH (OPTIONAL)   halved cherry tomatoes, dried cranberries or currants, toasted chopped pecans, sprigs of fresh dill

1.   Heat a stovetop grill pan over high heat. Brush one side of each chicken breast with about half of the oil. Reduce the heat to medium-high and arrange the chicken on the

grill, oiled sides down; cook for about 5 minutes. Brush the top surfaces with the remaining oil; turn and continue to cook for about 5 minutes or until the chicken is lightly browned and thoroughly cooked.

2. Transfer the chicken to a plate and sprinkle with pepper; set aside.

3. Meanwhile, toss together the rice, carrot, cucumber, bell pepper, scallions, and parsley in a medium bowl.

4. Whisk together the vinaigrette ingredients in a small bowl or measuring cup. Adjust the seasoning to taste.

5. Add $^1/_4$ cup of the vinaigrette to the rice mixture; toss.

6. When ready to serve, spoon the rice mixture onto four plates lined with lettuce. Slice the chicken diagonally into thin strips; arrange atop the rice. Whisk the remaining vinaigrette; drizzle over the salads.

PER SERVING: Cal 499/Prot 40.7g/Carb 49.4g/Fat 15.4g/Chol 87mg/Sod 103mg

ADVANCE PREPARATION   The day they are to be served, grill the chicken and prepare the rice mixture in advance; cover and refrigerate separately. Assemble the salads and drizzle with the remaining vinaigrette just before serving.

Variations

- Substitute other rice for all or part of the wild rice (up to 2 cups total). Try brown rice, white rice, or a combination.

- Substitute other chopped vegetables for the carrot, cucumber, or red bell pepper (up to 2 cups total). Try yellow squash or green bell pepper.

> ### TIP
>
> Dill is a sharply aromatic herb with a mild, lemony taste. When using fresh dill, cut the feathery dill tips with scissors. Dried dill is acceptable, but its flavor is stronger than fresh, so use it in moderation.

grilled
chicken and pear salad
with hazelnut vinaigrette

Makes 4 servings

The pronounced flavor of hazelnut oil is especially pleasing on bitter greens such as Belgian endive; other greens it complements include curly endive, dandelion greens, or escarole.

1 tablespoon olive oil, divided

1 pound boneless skinless chicken breast halves

1 large ripe pear (at room temperature), peeled, cored, and halved lengthwise, each half cut into $3/8$-inch-thick slices (see Tip)

Hazelnut Vinaigrette

$1/4$ cup red wine vinegar

3 tablespoons hazelnut oil

1 tablespoon extra-virgin olive oil

1 teaspoon Dijon mustard

$1/8$ teaspoon pepper, or to taste

Pinch of salt, or to taste

To Complete the Recipe

20 leaves Belgian endive (about 2 heads)

12 leaves leaf lettuce

Dash of pepper, or to taste

GARNISH (OPTIONAL) crumbled feta cheese, toasted hazelnuts, sprigs of fresh watercress

1. Heat a stovetop grill pan over high heat. Brush one side of each chicken breast with about 1 teaspoon of the oil. Reduce the heat to medium-high and arrange the chicken on the grill, oiled sides down; cook for about 5 minutes. Brush the top surfaces with about 1 teaspoon of the oil; turn and continue to cook for about 5 minutes or until the chicken is lightly browned and thoroughly cooked.

2. Transfer the chicken to a plate and cover to keep warm.

3. Meanwhile, whisk together the vinaigrette ingredients in a small bowl. Adjust the seasonings to taste. Set aside.

4. Lightly brush the pear slices with the remaining 1 teaspoon of oil, and cook on the preheated grill for about 10 to 15 minutes or just until the grill markings become light brown. Transfer to a plate and set aside.

5. To assemble the salads, arrange the endive and leaf lettuce on four salad plates. Slice the chicken into thin strips; arrange atop the greens along with the pear slices. Whisk the remaining vinaigrette; drizzle about 2 tablespoons over each salad. Sprinkle with pepper, garnish, and serve while the chicken is warm.

PER SERVING: Cal 339/Prot 33.2g/Carb 7.7g/Fat 19.5g/Chol 87mg/Sod 108mg

ADVANCE PREPARATION   The Hazelnut Vinaigrette will keep for up to 1 week in a tightly closed container in the refrigerator. Early on the day it is to be served, the chicken can be grilled and refrigerated. Grill the pear just before serving, or assemble the salads using uncooked pear slices. (Previously grilled pear slices darken and become limp.)

> **TIP**
>
> Buy pears when they are firm, but not rock-hard, and ripen them on your kitchen counter in a paper bag; this may require 2 to 7 days. Once they are ripe, they will keep for 3 to 5 days in the refrigerator. Most pears do not show ripeness with a color change because they ripen from the inside out; the stem ends yielding slightly to pressure indicate ripeness. Slightly underripe pears are the best for cooking and baking. It is not necessary to peel pears before using; but if they are peeled, they should be dipped in acidulated water (water with a small amount of lemon, lime, or orange juice added) to prevent the flesh from browning.

cashew
chicken salad
with cilantro vinaigrette

Makes 4 servings

In my opinion, this is the most stunning salad in this book, especially when served on festive orange plates. And the blend of flavors is pretty hard to beat, too. This is definitely my choice for do-ahead summer entertaining when nectarines are at their peak of flavor. During the winter, I substitute oranges.

1 tablespoon canola or safflower oil

1 pound boneless skinless chicken breast halves

Dash of pepper, or to taste

Cilantro Vinaigrette

1/4 cup fresh orange juice

2 tablespoons canola or safflower oil

1 tablespoon red wine vinegar

1 teaspoon Dijon mustard

1 teaspoon sugar

To Complete the Recipe

1/2 cup roasted salted cashews

8 cups shredded romaine lettuce (1 medium head)

2 nectarines (at room temperature), pitted and cut into 1/2-inch cubes

1 red bell pepper, cut into 1/2-inch squares

2 medium scallions, finely chopped

1/4 teaspoon hot pepper sauce, or to taste

Dash of pepper, or to taste

1/4 cup coarsely chopped fresh cilantro (do not substitute dried cilantro); (see Tip)

GARNISH (OPTIONAL) freshly ground black pepper, sprigs of fresh cilantro

1. Heat a stovetop grill pan over high heat. Brush one side of each chicken breast with about half of the oil. Reduce the heat to medium-high and arrange the chicken on the grill, oiled sides down; cook for about 5 minutes. Brush the top surfaces with the remaining oil; turn and continue to cook for about 5 minutes or until the chicken is lightly browned and thoroughly cooked.

2. Transfer the chicken to a plate and sprinkle with pepper; cut into 1-inch pieces. Refrigerate to cool.

3. Meanwhile, whisk together the vinaigrette ingredients (except the cilantro) in a small bowl or measuring cup until the sugar is dissolved. Stir in the cilantro. Adjust the seasonings to taste. Set aside.

4. Toss together the chicken, nectarines, bell pepper, scallions, and cashews in a medium bowl. Whisk the vinaigrette, add to the salad, and toss again.

5. To assemble the servings, arrange beds of the shredded romaine lettuce on four large salad plates or in large, shallow bowls. Top each with a mound of the salad mixture.

> **TIP**
>
> Cilantro, often sold as "fresh coriander" or "Chinese parsley," has a distinctive pungent flavor and fragrance, which lends itself well to highly spiced foods. Choose leaves with a bright, even color and no sign of wilting. The leaves are often used uncooked; if adding to a cooked recipe, do so near the end of the cooking period to retain full flavor. The dried leaves lack the distinctive flavor and are an unacceptable substitution. "Ground coriander" is made from the ground seeds and serves a different purpose in cooking.

PER SERVING: Cal 426/Prot 37.9g/Carb 21g/Fat 21.1g/Chol 87mg/Sod 90mg

ADVANCE PREPARATION The Cilantro Vinaigrette will keep for up to 2 days in a tightly closed container in the refrigerator. Early on the day it is to be served, the chicken can be grilled and refrigerated; if necessary, the salad mixture can also be tossed together. For the best texture, add the cashews just before serving.

Variations

- Substitute other fruit for the nectarines. Try 3 or 4 pitted apricots or 2 seedless oranges.
- Add up to 1/4 cup additional vegetables, such as finely chopped celery or green bell pepper.

grilled
chicken salad
with **grapefruit-peanut vinaigrette**

Makes 4 servings

This warm chicken salad is always a hit year-round but seems especially appropriate in the winter when grapefruit are at their juicy best and many other fruits are either unavailable or of poor quality. Roasted peanut oil gives the vinaigrette its outstanding aroma and flavor.

1 tablespoon roasted peanut oil (see Tips), divided

1 pound boneless skinless chicken breast halves

Dash of pepper, or to taste

Grapefruit-Peanut Vinaigrette

$1/2$ cup fresh grapefruit juice

2 tablespoons roasted peanut oil

$1/2$ teaspoon pepper, or to taste

To Complete the Recipe

8 cups romaine lettuce torn into 2-inch pieces (1 medium head)

1 seedless red grapefruit, peeled, halved vertically, and cut into $1/4$-inch-thick slices (see Tips)

1 red bell pepper, cut into 2-inch-long by $1/4$-inch-wide strips

$1/4$ cup coarsely chopped dry-roasted unsalted peanuts

GARNISH (OPTIONAL)   freshly ground black pepper, sprigs of fresh cilantro

1. Heat a stovetop grill pan over high heat. Brush one side of each chicken breast with about half of the peanut oil. Reduce the heat to medium-high and arrange the chicken on the grill, oiled sides down; cook for about 5 minutes. Brush the top surfaces with the remaining oil; turn and continue to cook for about 5 minutes or until the chicken is lightly browned and thoroughly cooked.

2. Transfer the chicken to a plate, sprinkle with pepper, and cover to keep warm.

3. Meanwhile, whisk together the vinaigrette ingredients in a small bowl or measuring cup. Adjust the seasoning to taste.

4. Toss the lettuce with $1/4$ cup of the vinaigrette in a large salad bowl. Divide among four large salad bowls or plates.

5. Slice the chicken into $1/2$-inch-wide diagonal strips; arrange atop the greens. Surround the chicken with the grapefruit slices and bell pepper strips. Whisk with the remaining vinaigrette; drizzle over the salads. Sprinkle with peanuts and serve immediately while the chicken is warm.

PER SERVING: Cal 379/Prot 37.8g/Carb 17.7g/Fat 17.4g/Chol 87mg/Sod 81mg

ADVANCE PREPARATION   The Grapefruit-Peanut Vinaigrette will keep for up to 2 days in a tightly closed container in the refrigerator. Early on the day it is to be served, the chicken can be grilled and refrigerated. Assemble the salads with the vinaigrette just before serving.

> ## TIPS
>
> - Grapefruit come in white (actually yellow), pink, and red varieties; all three are similar in flavor and texture. Choose grapefruit that have a thin, fine-textured, brightly colored skin. The heavier they are for their size, the juicier they will be. Do not store grapefruit at room temperature for more than a day or two. They will keep for up to 2 weeks when wrapped in a plastic bag and refrigerated in the vegetable drawer.
>
> - Roasted peanut oil is made from peanuts that are dry-roasted prior to pressing; the aroma and flavor are far superior to other peanut oils. Roasted peanut oil is available in many supermarkets.

Variations

- Substitute orange juice and orange slices for the grapefruit juice and grapefruit slices.

- Serve the chicken chilled or at room temperature.

chicken fruit platter
with orange-ginger
dressing

Makes 4 servings

Orange-Ginger Dressing is a splendid sauce. Count on it to turn nearly any fruit into a luxury. Serve this refreshing salad for lunch or a light dinner accompanied by peasant bread or your favorite kind of muffin.

2 teaspoons canola or safflower oil, divided

12 ounces boneless skinless chicken
   breast halves

1 cup thinly sliced celery

Orange-Ginger Dressing

$1/2$ cup low-fat plain yogurt

$1/4$ cup frozen orange juice concentrate,
   thawed

1 tablespoon finely minced crystallized
   ginger (see Tip)

1 teaspoon sugar

To Complete the Recipe

4 leaves leaf lettuce

$1/2$ medium cantaloupe, peeled, seeded,
   and cut into 8 wedges

$1/4$ medium honeydew melon, peeled,
   seeded, and cut into 4 wedges

4 small clusters of seedless red grapes

GARNISH (OPTIONAL)   toasted sliced almonds

1. Heat a stovetop grill pan over high heat. Brush one side of each chicken breast with about half of the oil. Reduce the heat to medium-high and arrange the chicken on the grill, oiled sides down; continue to cook for about 5 minutes. Brush the top surfaces

with the remaining oil; turn and cook for about 5 minutes or until the chicken is lightly browned and thoroughly cooked.

2. Transfer the chicken to a plate; cut into 2-inch-long by $^1/_2$-inch-wide strips.
   Refrigerate to cool.

3. Meanwhile, stir together the dressing ingredients in a medium bowl until the sugar is
   dissolved.

4. Remove $^1/_4$ cup of the dressing and set aside. Add the chicken and celery to the dressing remaining in the bowl; toss until well combined.

5. To serve, mound the chicken salad atop lettuce leaves on four plates; surround with the
   cantaloupe and honeydew wedges and clusters of grapes. Whisk the remaining dressing; drizzle about 1 tablespoon over the melon wedges.

PER SERVING: Cal 315/Prot 29.1g/Carb 37.7g/Fat 5.3g/Chol 67mg/Sod 122mg

ADVANCE PREPARATION   The Orange-Ginger Dressing will keep for up to
2 days in a tightly closed container in the refrigerator. The chicken salad can
be made and refrigerated early on the day it is to be served.

Variations

- Substitute other fruit for the cantaloupe or honeydew melon. Try
  pineapple slices or fresh peach or apricot wedges.

- Rather than serving as a salad, stuff the chicken salad mixture into
  pita bread pockets.

> **TIP**
>
> Crystallized (or candied) ginger has been
> cooked in a sugar syrup and coated with
> coarse sugar. This sweet ginger, which is
> generally used as a confection or added to
> desserts, plays a different role in cooking
> than fresh ginger.

warm
walnut-chicken
salad

Makes 4 servings

The distinctively, seductively nutty flavor and fragrance of walnut oil is the essence of this salad. Serve it over romaine, or try substituting a mixture of distinctive greens, such as endive, chicory, or escarole.

Walnut Vinaigrette

1/4 cup red wine vinegar

1/4 cup walnut oil (see Tips)

1 tablespoon fresh lemon juice

2 teaspoons Dijon mustard

1/4 cup minced fresh flat-leaf parsley

1/8 teaspoon pepper, or to taste

To Complete the Recipe

2 teaspoons olive oil

1 pound boneless skinless chicken breast halves, cut into 3-inch-long by 1/2-inch-wide strips

8 cups romaine lettuce torn into 2-inch pieces (1 medium head)

2 medium scallions, finely chopped

4 plum tomatoes, each cut into 6 wedges

1 tablespoon red wine vinegar

1 tablespoon minced fresh flat-leaf parsley

1 tablespoon minced fresh tarragon (or 1 teaspoon dried tarragon)

Dash of pepper, or to taste

GARNISH (OPTIONAL)   toasted pine nuts or toasted chopped walnuts or hazelnuts (see Tips)

1.   To prepare the vinaigrette: Whisk together the vinegar, oil, lemon juice, and mustard in a small bowl. Stir in the parsley and pepper. Adjust the seasoning to taste. Set aside.

2. Heat the oil in a medium nonstick skillet over medium-high heat. Add the chicken; cook, stirring occasionally for about 5 minutes or until it is lightly browned and cooked through.

3. Meanwhile, mound the lettuce onto 4 serving plates; sprinkle with the scallions. Arrange the tomato wedges around the edges. Set aside.

4. Remove the skillet from the heat; stir in the vinegar, parsley, tarragon, and pepper. Adjust the seasoning to taste.

5. Arrange the warm chicken strips atop the lettuce. Whisk the vinaigrette and drizzle over the chicken, lettuce, and tomato wedges (about 3 tablespoons per salad). Serve immediately.

PER SERVING: Cal 348/Prot 35g/Carb 8.9g/Fat 19.9g/Chol 87mg/Sod 95mg

ADVANCE PREPARATION   The Walnut Vinaigrette can be made in advance and refrigerated for up to 2 days. The salads can be assembled, refrigerated for several hours, and served chilled or at room temperature. Drizzle with the vinaigrette just before serving.

Variations

- Add up to ¼ cup chopped red bell stemmed pepper to the romaine-scallion layer. Add about 6 blanched stemmed snow peas to each salad alternating with the tomato wedges.

- Allow the chicken to cool; toss with the scallions, plum tomatoes, and the vinaigrette. Serve on salad plates or stuff the mixture into pita bread pockets.

> ### TIPS
>
> - Walnut oil has a pleasant, nutty taste and is used mainly for salads, rather than as a cooking medium. Because walnut oil turns rancid quickly, refrigerate after opening; it will keep for up to 3 months.
>
> - Toasting will enhance the flavor of most nuts. To toast nuts on the stovetop, put them in a dry skillet over medium heat. Stir and toss them for about 4 to 5 minutes or until they are golden brown. If you prefer, nuts can be toasted on a baking sheet in a 375°F oven for about 4 to 5 minutes, stirring frequently.
>
> - Because of their high fat content, nuts quickly become rancid at room temperature. Shelled nuts can be refrigerated in an airtight container for up to 4 months or frozen for up to 6 months. To freshen the flavor, spread the nuts on a baking sheet and heat in a 150°F oven for a few minutes.

grilled
chicken salad
with herbed tomato vinaigrette

Makes 4 servings

Served on a bed of wilted greens and drizzled with Herbed Tomato Vinaigrette, this chicken salad will delight the palate and excite the eye. If possible, use fresh herbs both in the dressing and as a garnish.

1 tablespoon olive oil, divided

1 pound boneless skinless chicken breast halves

Dash of pepper, or to taste

Herbed Tomato Vinaigrette

2 tablespoons red wine vinegar

2 tablespoons extra-virgin olive oil

$1/2$ cup water

1 tablespoon tomato paste

1 tablespoon minced fresh basil (or
 $1/2$ teaspoon dried basil)

1 tablespoon minced fresh oregano (or
 $1/2$ teaspoon dried oregano)

$1/2$ teaspoon minced garlic

$1/4$ teaspoon pepper, or to taste

To Complete the Recipe

8 cups kale leaves (this yields 4 cups
 after steaming); (see Tips)

$1/2$ cup frozen corn, thawed

GARNISH (OPTIONAL) freshly ground black pepper, sprigs of fresh basil or oregano

1. Heat a stovetop grill pan over high heat. Brush one side of each chicken breast with about half of the olive oil. Reduce the heat to medium-high and arrange the chicken on the grill, oiled sides down; cook for about 5 minutes. Brush the top surfaces with the remaining oil; turn and continue to cook for about 5 minutes or until the chicken is lightly browned and thoroughly cooked.

2. Transfer the chicken to a plate, sprinkle with pepper, and cover to keep warm.

3. Meanwhile, whisk together the vinaigrette ingredients in a small bowl. Adjust the seasoning to taste. Set aside.

4. Rinse the kale leaves in cool water; do not dry. Drop them into a medium saucepan over medium-high heat. Cook, covered, without additional water except for the drops that cling to the leaves. Reduce the heat to medium and steam for about 3 to 4 minutes or until wilted. Remove the pan from the heat; keep covered.

5. Slice the chicken into 1/2-inch-wide diagonal strips.

6. To assemble the salads, spread the kale on each plate. Top with the chicken strips. Whisk the vinaigrette before drizzling it over the salads. Sprinkle with the corn.

PER SERVING: Cal 315/Prot 36.2g/Carb 13.3g/Fat 13g/Chol 87mg/Sod 106mg

Variation

- Substitute frisée for the kale (see Tips).

TIPS

- Kale is a member of the cabbage family. Ornamental varieties come in shades of blue and purple. For steaming, choose the dark green kale, avoiding any limp or yellowing leaves. Store it in the coldest section of the refrigerator for no longer than 2 or 3 days; after that, the flavor becomes quite strong and the leaves turn limp. Because the center stalk is tough, remove it before cooking.

- Frisée is a member of the chicory family. It has delicate, curly leaves that range in color from yellow-white to yellow-green. Choose crisp, unwilted leaves; refrigerate in a plastic bag for up to 5 days. Frisée has a mildly bitter flavor. It can be eaten cooked or raw; it is often an ingredient in the mix of greens called mesclun.

warm
raspberry-walnut
chicken salad

Makes 4 servings

Serve this salad as a special summer treat when sweet fresh raspberries are readily available. In the winter, I compose the plates with additional orange slices or substitute pear slices.

1 tablespoon olive oil, divided

1 pound boneless skinless chicken breast halves

Dash of pepper, or to taste

Raspberry-Walnut Vinaigrette

$^1/_2$ cup raspberry vinegar (see Tips)

$^1/_4$ cup walnut oil

2 tablespoons fresh lemon juice

2 tablespoons minced fresh flat-leaf parsley

1 teaspoon Dijon mustard

$^1/_8$ teaspoon pepper, or to taste

To Complete the Recipe

8 cups mesclun (mixed baby greens)

2 medium scallions, finely chopped

12 leaves Belgian endive (about 1 head)

2 large oranges, peeled, seeded, each cut crosswise into 6 thin slices (see Tips)

1 cup raspberries (omit if fresh are unavailable)

GARNISH (OPTIONAL)   toasted coarsely chopped walnuts, chèvre cheese

1. Heat a stovetop grill pan over high heat. Brush one side of each chicken breast with about half of the olive oil. Reduce the heat to medium-high and arrange the chicken on the grill, oiled sides down; cook for about 5 minutes. Brush the top surfaces with the remaining oil; turn and cook for about 5 more minutes or until the chicken is lightly browned and thoroughly cooked.

2. Transfer the chicken to a plate, sprinkle with pepper, and cover to keep warm.

3. Meanwhile, whisk together the vinaigrette ingredients in a small saucepan. Adjust the seasoning to taste. Heat the vinaigrette over medium heat until it is warm but not hot (it will evaporate if permitted to boil). Remove the pan from the heat; cover and set aside.

4. Toss together the mesclun and the scallions in a large bowl. Stir the warm vinaigrette, add $1/4$ cup to the greens, and toss again.

5. To assemble the salads, spread the dressed greens on four dinner plates. Diagonally slice the warm chicken into thin strips. Top the greens with a composed arrangement of chicken strips, endive leaves, orange slices, and raspberries. Stir the remaining warm vinaigrette, drizzle over the salads, and serve immediately.

PER SERVING: Cal 399/Prot 36.3g/Carb 18.6g/Fat 19.9g/Chol 87mg/Sod 95mg

ADVANCE PREPARATION The Raspberry-Walnut Vinaigrette will keep for up to 2 days in a tightly closed container in the refrigerator. The chicken can be grilled in advance and chilled or brought to room temperature. Assemble the salads and drizzle with room temperature vinaigrette just before serving.

> ## TIPS
>
> - To peel an orange, immerse it in boiling water for 5 minutes, cool for a few minutes, then peel. The white membrane, which imparts a bitter flavor, can be removed more easily using this method.
>
> - Fruit vinegars are made by adding soft fruits and their concentrates to mild vinegars, most often white wine vinegar. Sugar and liqueurs are sometimes added to counteract the acidity; colorings may be added to enhance the vinegar's appearance. The most common varieties are raspberry, blueberry, blackberry, and black currant. Available in many supermarkets and gourmet shops, these products add a special touch to dressings destined for both green and fruit salads; and they lend character to marinades.

warm gingered chicken
stir-fry salad
with ginger-soy vinaigrette

Makes 4 servings

Here, a colorful stir-fried mixture is served warm on a bed of greens, with a gingered vinaigrette. For variety, substitute Chinese wheat-flour noodles for the greens.

Ginger-Soy Vinaigrette

$1/3$ cup white rice vinegar

2 tablespoons canola or safflower oil

1 tablespoon low-sodium soy sauce

2 teaspoons toasted sesame seeds (see Tips)

1 teaspoon Dijon mustard

1 teaspoon finely minced fresh ginger

$1/2$ teaspoon minced garlic

$1/2$ teaspoon pepper, or to taste

To Complete the Recipe

4 cups stemmed salad spinach leaves

2 tablespoons canola or safflower oil, divided

8 ounces boneless skinless chicken breast halves, cut into 2-inch by $1/2$-inch strips

4 cups broccoli florets

3 carrots, cut into 2-inch-long by $1/4$-inch-wide strips

2 medium scallions, coarsely chopped

1 teaspoon minced garlic

1. Whisk together the vinaigrette ingredients in a measuring cup or small bowl. Adjust the seasoning to taste. Set aside.

2. Arrange a bed of spinach leaves on four dinner plates.

154

3. Heat 1 tablespoon of the oil in a large nonstick skillet or wok over medium-high heat. Add the chicken; stir-fry for about 5 minutes or until it is lightly browned and cooked through.

4. With a slotted spoon, transfer the chicken to a bowl and cover to keep warm.

5. Heat the remaining 1 tablespoon of oil in the pan. Add the broccoli and carrots; stir-fry for about 4 minutes or until the vegetables are crisp-tender. Add the scallions and garlic; continue to cook only until they are softened. Reduce the heat to medium; stir in the chicken strips.

6. Whisk the vinaigrette and add $1/4$ cup to the chicken-vegetable mixture; stir gently until just warm (the vinaigrette will evaporate if permitted to boil).

7. To serve, spoon the stir-fried mixture over the spinach leaves. Drizzle each serving with about 1 tablespoon vinaigrette.

PER SERVING: Cal 295/Prot 21.9g/Carb 14.7g/Fat 16.5g/Chol 44mg/Sod 265mg

ADVANCE PREPARATION   The Ginger-Soy Vinaigrette will keep for up to 1 week in a tightly closed container in the refrigerator. The stir-fried chicken and vegetables can be prepared in advance on the day they are to be served. Assemble the chilled salads with the remaining vinaigrette just before serving.

TIPS

- Because they contain oil, sesame seeds become rancid at room temperature; store them in the refrigerator for up to 6 months or in the freezer for up to 1 year.

- To toast sesame seeds, put them in a dry, nonstick skillet over medium-high heat for 3 to 5 minutes. Toss constantly and watch closely, removing the seeds from the pan when they are lightly browned. As an alternative, spread the seeds on an ungreased baking sheet and bake in a 350°F oven. Shake the pan or stir occasionally for about 10 minutes or until the seeds are lightly browned. Either method will give the seeds a nutty flavor. It takes the same amount of time to toast 1 tablespoon or $1/2$ cup—so toast extra seeds, store them in an airtight container, and refrigerate or freeze.

chicken
stir-fry salad
with sesame-orange dressing

Makes 4 servings

Chinese wheat-flour noodles tossed with Sesame-Orange Dressing form a delectable founda-tion for vegetables and chicken, all flavored with a hint of citrus.

Sesame-Orange Dressing

$1/2$ teaspoon orange zest	1 teaspoon low-sodium soy sauce
$1/2$ cup fresh orange juice	1 teaspoon dark sesame oil
1 tablespoon canola or safflower oil	$1/2$ teaspoon toasted sesame seeds
2 teaspoons sugar	$1/8$ teaspoon pepper, or to taste

To Complete the Recipe

1 tablespoon canola or safflower oil	2 medium scallions, coarsely chopped
12 ounces boneless skinless chicken breast halves, cut into 2-inch by $1/2$-inch strips	1 teaspoon minced garlic
	4 ounces Chinese wheat-flour noodles
4 cups asparagus in 2-inch-long pieces (see Tip)	

GARNISH (OPTIONAL)   freshly ground black pepper, toasted sesame seeds, orange slices

1. Bring a large saucepan of unsalted water to a boil over high heat.

2. While the water is coming to a boil, combine the dressing ingredients in a small bowl or measuring cup, whisking until the sugar is dissolved. Adjust the seasoning to taste. Set aside.

3. Heat the oil in a large nonstick skillet or wok over medium-high heat. Add the chicken and asparagus; stir-fry for about 5 minutes, adding the scallions and garlic during the last minute. The chicken should be lightly browned and cooked through, the asparagus crisp-tender. Reduce the heat to low. Whisk the dressing; add about $1/4$ cup to the stir-fried mixture, and stir gently until warm (the vinaigrette will evaporate if permitted to boil).

4. While the chicken and vegetables are cooking, cook the noodles in the boiling water for about 3 minutes, or according to package instructions, until noodles are *al dente*. As they cook, break the noodles apart with a fork. Drain well; rinse with cool water, drain again, and pour into a medium bowl. Whisk the remaining $1/4$ cup of the dressing, add to the noodles, and toss.

5. To serve, place a bed of noodles on each of four plates; top with the warm, stir-fried chicken and vegetables.

PER SERVING: Cal 314/Prot 31.3g/Carb 21.1g/Fat 11.6g/Chol 75mg/Sod 109mg

ADVANCE PREPARATION   The Sesame-Orange Dressing will keep for up to 2 days in a tightly closed container in the refrigerator. The noodles, as well as the stir-fried chicken and vegetables, can be prepared early on the day they are to be served; toss with the vinaigrette and refrigerate separately. Assemble the chilled salads just before serving.

Variation

• Substitute other vegetables for the asparagus (up to 4 cups total). Try carrot strips, broccoli florets, red bell pepper strips, or stemmed snow peas.

> **TIP**
>
> Asparagus is at its best in the early spring. Choose green spears with firm stalks; the tips should be tightly closed and have a lavender hue. Slender stalks are more tender. Uniformity in size and shape is important for even cooking; if you can't find thin asparagus, halve the thicker stalks. To store, wrap asparagus in a plastic bag and store in the vegetable crisper; use within 2 to 3 days. Do not clean the asparagus until you are ready to cook it. If wilted, stand the stalks in a jar filled with about 2 inches of very cold water. Cover with a plastic bag, fasten, and refrigerate for 1 to 2 hours before cooking.

Warm Chicken and Peach Summer Salad

warm
chicken and peach
summer salad

Makes 4 servings

Nothing says "summer" better than fresh, juicy peaches and sweet, luscious blueberries. Make this salad when fruits are at their peak, and enjoy summer dining at its best.

1 tablespoon olive oil, divided

1 pound boneless skinless chicken breast
halves

Peach Vinaigrette

1 peach, peeled, pitted, and chopped

2 tablespoons fresh lemon juice

1 tablespoon white rice vinegar (see Tips)

1 teaspoon honey

Dash of pepper, or to taste

To Complete the Recipe

4 cups mesclun (mixed baby greens)

2 tablespoons extra-virgin olive oil

Dash of salt

2 peaches (at room temperature), peeled,
pitted, and cut into 8 wedges each

Dash of freshly gound black pepper, or to
taste

$1/2$ cup blueberries (omit if fresh are
unavailable); (see Tips)

1. Heat a stovetop grill pan over high heat. Brush one side of each chicken breast with about half of the oil. Reduce the heat to medium-high and arrange the chicken on the grill, oiled sides down; cook for about 5 minutes. Brush the top surfaces with the

(continues)

159

remaining oil; turn and continue to cook for about 5 minutes or until the chicken is lightly browned and thoroughly cooked.

2. Transfer the chicken to a plate and cover to keep warm.

3. Meanwhile, process all of the vinaigrette ingredients in a blender until smooth. Adjust the seasoning to taste. Set aside.

4. Toss the mesclun with the extra-virgin olive oil and a dash of salt in a large salad bowl. Arrange the greens on four salad plates.

5. Diagonally slice the chicken breasts into $1/2$-inch-wide strips and arrange them atop the greens. Arrange the peach wedges next to the chicken strips on the plate. Drizzle the vinaigrette over the salads. Sprinkle with pepper and top with the blueberries. Serve immediately while the chicken is warm.

PER SERVING: Cal 309/Prot 34.2g/Carb 14.1g/Fat 12.7g/Chol 87mg/Sod 110mg

ADVANCE PREPARATION   Early on the day it is to be served, the chicken can be grilled and refrigerated. Make the Peach Vinaigrette and assemble the salads just before serving.

Variation

• Substitute other fruit for the fresh peaches in the vinaigrette and the salad. Try nectarines or unsweetened, canned peach halves (you'll need two 16-ounce cans), or fresh raspberries. A combination of berries also works well.

TIPS

• When buying blueberries, look for those that are full and uniform in shape and deep blue in color. They should have a powdery look, called "bloom," which is a sign of freshness. Refrigerated berries will keep for about 1 week; wash them just before using.

• Chinese or Japanese rice vinegar, made from fermented rice, has a low acid content and is milder and sweeter than most Western vinegars. The colors range from the mildest white to a sweet red and the sweetest, purple-black. "Seasoned" white rice vinegar contains rice vinegar, sugar, and salt.

chapter 4

Chicken Soups

CHICKEN SOUP HAS ESTABLISHED QUITE A REPUTATION

as the quintessential cure-all comfort food. Eating chicken

soup while developing these recipes brought back childhood

memories of being home from school with some malady or

other, made better—or so it seemed—by Mom bringing

chicken noodle soup to my bedside. As an adult, I can still

attest from personal experience that the restorative proper-

ties of chicken soup are genuine. Best of all, it tastes good.

There is something especially satisfying about soups that are homemade. They taste the best, for sure. They fill your kitchen with fragrant aromas. I have never found a canned soup that can compare. But most people think made-from-scratch chicken soup requires hours of simmering in quantities large enough to feed the neighborhood. The fact is, not all soups require hours on the stove; and why settle for opening a can or dropping a bag into boiling water when each of the recipes in this chapter can go from kettle to bowl in 15 minutes or less?

The godsend that makes delicious homemade chicken soups possible in no time is good-quality, canned or aseptically packaged chicken broth. Many excellent brands can be found in the supermarket, some with reduced (or even eliminated) sodium and fat. Although I prefer canned broth, I keep cubes and powdered forms on hand, too. (Use cubes and broth powder if you need just a small amount of chicken broth. Some are very salty; but these products are also available unsalted or with reduced salt.) After all, the foundation for every great pot of soup is the broth—and this is especially true for soups made with few ingredients.

The personality of the soup comes from the chicken, vegetables, and herbs. Since virtually every cuisine has its distinctive "chicken soup," the possibilities are endless. Italians add pasta, beans, abundant herbs, and a garnish of freshly grated Parmesan cheese. Asian soups are flavored with soy sauce and sesame oil and may include soba noodles or eggs.

It is easy to make these healthful soups without a lot of fat, and carefully selected herbs and spices showcase the flavors of the chicken and vegetables, eliminating the need for much salt. (Unless specified, my recipes call for regular chicken broth; I do not add additional salt.) Since can sizes vary, amounts are provided by cups. It is usually not necessary for quantities to be exact; if you don't have quite enough broth, you can add dehydrated chicken broth powder dissolved in water—or just plain water.

Certain other techniques and ingredient choices also help eliminate hours of simmering and ensure first-rate flavor. Firm vegetables can be cut into small pieces and then sautéed before the broth is added; sautéing carrots and onions will bring out their sweetness and add depth to the

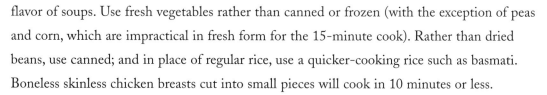

flavor of soups. Use fresh vegetables rather than canned or frozen (with the exception of peas and corn, which are impractical in fresh form for the 15-minute cook). Rather than dried beans, use canned; and in place of regular rice, use a quicker-cooking rice such as basmati. Boneless skinless chicken breasts cut into small pieces will cook in 10 minutes or less.

Like most soups, all of these recipes can be made in advance and refrigerated for a day or two before reheating on the stove or even in the microwave. Some of them probably could be frozen—but, personally, I'm convinced that freezing alters flavors. Refrigerating, however, in many cases actually helps blend and enhance the flavors, making these recipes wise choices if you care to plan ahead for days when you don't want to cook.

Soups are also ideal weekend fare when you are expecting guests, and they rate as crowd-pleasers! For entertaining, I often serve a hearty soup as an entrée, accompanied by a substantial salad and great bread. Pita Crisps (page 188) and Baked Tortilla Chips (page 187) make quick-to-prepare additions. These soup recipes each provide 4 substantial entrée servings, or 6 as a first course. They all can be doubled easily, but add only $1^1/_2$ times the amount of herbs and ingredients such as pepper and red pepper flakes; then taste and adjust the seasonings.

Keep in mind that soup recipes do not demand strict adherence—so relax. Improvise. Substitute your favorite herbs or the odds and ends of vegetables that you may have on hand. Add more (or less) chicken, and to give your soups a special touch, call on garnishes for extra interest, from a sprinkling of fresh herbs to homemade Herbed Croutons (page 132). You can break up the plain, flat surface of soup by adding almost any food that won't sink to the bottom of the bowl; this adds color and texture, too.

Although these soups are quick to prepare, the benefits are long-lived. Your kitchen will be filled with fragrant aromas, and in the winter, when the weather calls for comfort food, these hearty meals in a bowl are especially welcome. Actually, soups are some of my favorite comforts any time of the year.

chicken
noodle
soup

Makes 4 servings

Chicken noodle soup is everybody's favorite. For variety, however, in place of the noodles I sometimes substitute chicken-, mushroom-, or cheese-filled tortellini or ravioli to make a more filling entrée. For a lighter soup, I substitute orzo pasta (see Tips).

1 tablespoon olive oil

2 carrots, cut into $1/8$-inch-thick slices

$1/4$ cup coarsely chopped onion

1 ($49^{1}/2$-ounce) can chicken broth (6 cups)

8 ounces boneless skinless chicken breast halves, cut into 3-inch-long by 1-inch-wide strips

3 ribs celery, thinly sliced (also shred green tops)

2 tablespoons minced fresh flat-leaf parsley

$1/2$ teaspoon minced fresh thyme (or 2 teaspoons dried thyme)

$1/4$ teaspoon pepper, or to taste

1 bay leaf (see Tips)

2 cups wide egg noodles (3 ounces)

1. Heat the oil in a large saucepan or Dutch oven over medium-high heat. Add the carrots and onion; cook, stirring occasionally, for about 2 minutes or until the carrots are crisp-tender and the onion is translucent and not browned.

2. Add the chicken broth; increase the heat to high.

3. When the broth comes to a boil, stir in the remaining ingredients. When the liquid returns to a boil, reduce the heat to medium; cover and cook for about 10 minutes or until the chicken is cooked through and the noodles are tender.

4. Remove the bay leaf and discard. Adjust the seasoning to taste.

PER SERVING: Cal 290/Prot 28.1g/Carb 25.7g/Fat 8.3g/Chol 69mg/Sod 1,240mg

ADVANCE PREPARATION   Chicken Noodle Soup will keep, covered and refrigerated, for up to 2 days.

Variations

- Add other vegetables, such as 2 or 3 cubed plum tomatoes, up to $1/4$ cup diced red bell pepper, or up to $1/2$ cup frozen peas.

- Substitute dill for the thyme.

- Substitute other pasta for the noodles. Try about 8 ounces tortellini or ravioli purchased in the refrigerator or freezer section of the supermarket. Cook in the soup for about 6 minutes, or according to package instructions. Since these products are more filling than noodles, you may want to reduce the amount of chicken.

- Substitute $1/2$ cup orzo pasta (see Tips) for the noodles; substitute 2 cups asparagus in 1-inch pieces for the carrots; substitute 2 leeks, halved and thinly sliced, for the onion; substitute tarragon for the thyme.

> ## TIPS
>
> - Bay leaf is an aromatic herb that comes from the evergreen bay laurel tree, native to the Mediterranean. Fresh bay leaves are rarely available, but dried bay leaves are found in most supermarkets. Store them in an airtight container in a cool, dark place for up to 6 months. Since overuse will make a dish bitter, use the leaves in moderation and always remove them before serving the dish.
>
> - Available in most supermarkets, orzo is a tiny, rice-shaped pasta. It can be used as a substitute for rice.

Chicken Soup Provençal

chicken
soup
provençal

Makes 4 servings

The secret to this soup is herbes de Provence, a mixture of herbs commonly used in the south of France. The blend, usually containing basil, fennel seed, marjoram, rosemary, sage, summer savory, thyme, and lavender, can be found in tiny clay crocks in many gourmet shops and in the spice section of many supermarkets.

1 tablespoon olive oil

2 carrots, diced

2 leeks (both white and tender green parts), finely chopped (about 2 cups); (see Tip)

1 teaspoon minced garlic

1 ($14^1/_2$-ounce) can chicken broth (2 cups)

1 (15-ounce) can cannellini beans, drained and rinsed

1 ($14^1/_2$-ounce) can plum (Italian) tomatoes, with juice

1 cup new potatoes in $^1/_2$-inch cubes

8 ounces boneless skinless chicken breast halves, cut into 1-inch-long by $^1/_2$-inch-wide strips

1 teaspoon herbes de Provence

$^1/_2$ teaspoon pepper

1. Heat the oil in a large saucepan or Dutch oven over medium-high heat. Add the carrots and leeks; cook, stirring occasionally, for about 2 minutes. Add the garlic; continue to cook, stirring constantly, for about 1 minute or until the vegetables are somewhat softened but not tender or browned.

(continues)

2. Stir in the remaining ingredients. Increase the heat to high; when the mixture comes to a boil, reduce the heat to medium. Cover and cook for about 10 minutes or until the chicken is cooked through and the vegetables are tender. Adjust the seasoning to taste.

PER SERVING: Cal 556/Prot 43.6g/Carb 80.9g/Fat 7.6g/Chol 44mg/Sod 622mg

ADVANCE PREPARATION   Chicken Soup Provençal will keep, covered and refrigerated, for up to 2 days.

TIP

Leeks, which look like giant scallions, are available year-round in most areas. Select those with crisp, bright green leaves and unblemished, thin, white portions; leeks not exceeding $1^1/_2$ inches in diameter will be the most tender and delicately flavored. Refrigerate them in a plastic bag for up to 5 days. Before using, trim the rootlets and leaf ends, slit the leeks from top to bottom, and wash thoroughly to remove the dirt and sand, which is often trapped between the leaf layers. Use both the white base and the tender portions of the green leaves.

curried
chicken and **rice**
soup

Makes 4 servings

This jazzed-up version of a good, basic chicken and rice soup is one of my favorites for lunch on a cold winter day; it is also light enough to serve as a first course any time of the year.

2 ($14^1/_2$-ounce) cans chicken broth (4 cups)

1 ($14^1/_2$-ounce) can stewed tomatoes, with juice

8 ounces boneless skinless chicken breasts, cut into $^1/_2$-inch squares

$^1/_3$ cup basmati rice

1 tablespoon minced fresh flat-leaf parsley

1 teaspoon curry powder, or to taste (see Tip)

1 teaspoon minced garlic

$^1/_2$ teaspoon dried thyme

$^1/_4$ teaspoon pepper, or to taste

> **TIP**
>
> Curry powder, a combination of many herbs and spices, is blended in literally thousands of versions. Domestic curry powders are usually quite mild. Imported brands are often more flavorful; some offer several choices labeled as mild, medium, or hot.

1. Stir together the chicken broth and stewed tomatoes with juice in a large saucepan or Dutch oven. Bring the mixture to a boil over high heat.

2. Stir in the remaining ingredients. When the liquid returns to a boil, reduce the heat to medium; cover and cook for about 10 minutes or until the chicken is cooked through and the rice is tender. Adjust the seasoning to taste.

PER SERVING: Cal 211/Prot 23.7g/Carb 20.4g/Fat 3.8g/Chol 44mg/Sod 1,074mg

ADVANCE PREPARATION   Curried Chicken and Rice Soup will keep, covered and refrigerated, for up to 2 days.

Variation

• Add up to 1 cup other vegetables, such as small broccoli florets or frozen peas (preferably baby peas).

169

chicken, **barley,** and vegetable soup

Makes 4 servings

With "quick-cooking" barley, this classic soup can easily be ready in 15 minutes.

1 tablespoon olive oil

2 carrots, cut into $1/8$-inch slices

1 ($49^1/2$-ounce) can chicken broth (6 cups)

8 ounces boneless skinless chicken breast
halves, cut into 1-inch-long by
$1/2$-inch-wide strips

2 ribs celery, thinly sliced (also shred tops)

$1/2$ cup quick-cooking pearl barley

$1/4$ cup finely chopped onion

$1/4$ cup minced fresh flat-leaf parsley

1 teaspoon dried thyme

1 bay leaf

$1/2$ teaspoon pepper, or to taste

1. Heat the oil in a large saucepan or Dutch oven over medium-high heat. Add the carrots; cook, stirring occasionally, for about 2 minutes or until they are crisp-tender.

2. Add the chicken broth; increase the heat to high.

3. When the broth comes to a boil, stir in the remaining ingredients. When the liquid returns to a boil, reduce the heat to medium; cover and cook for about 10 minutes or until the chicken is cooked through and the barley is tender.

4. Remove the bay leaf and discard. Adjust the seasoning to taste.

PER SERVING: Calories 282/Prot 27g/Carb 26.5g/Fat 7.6g/Chol 44mg/Sod 1,233mg

ADVANCE PREPARATION   Chicken, Barley, and Vegetable Soup will keep, covered and refrigerated, for up to 2 days.

two-potato
chicken soup
with **spinach**

Makes 4 servings

Who doesn't love potato soup? It's all the better made with chicken and two kinds of potatoes.
The pleasing blend of flavors is enhanced by the sweetness of the yam.

1 (49$\frac{1}{2}$-ounce) can chicken broth (6 cups)

8 ounces boneless skinless chicken breast
  halves, cut into 1-inch squares

2 cups coarsely shredded stemmed salad
  spinach leaves (see Tip)

1 medium yam, peeled and cut into 1-inch
  cubes (about 2 cups)

1 medium red-skinned potato, cut into
  1-inch cubes (about 1$\frac{1}{2}$ cups)

3 medium scallions, coarsely
  chopped

$\frac{1}{2}$ teaspoon dried rosemary,
  crushed

$\frac{1}{2}$ teaspoon pepper, or to taste

1. Pour the chicken broth into a large saucepan or Dutch oven; bring
   to a boil over high heat.

2. Stir in the remaining ingredients. When the liquid returns to a boil,
   reduce the heat to medium; cover and cook for about 10 minutes
   or until the chicken is cooked through and the potatoes are tender.
   Adjust the seasoning to taste.

PER SERVING: Calories 255/Prot 26.4g/Carb 28.4g/Fat 4g/Chol 44mg/Sod 1,228mg

---

TIP

When buying fresh spinach, look for springy, bright leaves and short stems. In general, the smaller the spinach leaves, the more tender and more delicately flavored the vegetable will be. Salad spinach, sold in most supermarkets, is tender spinach leaves that have been prewashed before packaging and are ready to use uncooked. Before using other leaves, be sure to rinse under cold running water to remove any sand, then dry. Remove the stems before using all spinach. Spinach will keep for only 2 to 4 days, so store it in a sealed plastic bag in the vegetable crisper, and use it soon. If it seems wilted, wrap the leaves in moist paper towels and refrigerate to revive.

ADVANCE PREPARATION   Two-Potato Chicken Soup with Spinach will keep, covered and refrigerated, for up to 2 days.

shiitake
mushroom
soup

Makes 4 servings

In traditional Buddhist cultures where meat is not eaten, shiitake mushrooms are often used as a sublime substitute. Spring and autumn are the seasons when fresh shiitakes are most plentiful. At other times, if necessary, use dried shiitake mushrooms (see Tips).

2 (14$^{1}/_{2}$-ounce) cans chicken broth
(4 cups)

4 ounces fresh shiitake mushroom caps,
cut into $^{1}/_{4}$-inch-wide strips (see Tips)

4 ounces boneless skinless chicken breast
halves, cut into 1-inch-long by
$^{1}/_{4}$-inch-wide strips

$^{1}/_{2}$ cup coarsely shredded carrot

1 medium scallion, coarsely chopped

2 tablespoons cold water

1 tablespoon cornstarch

1 tablespoon low-sodium soy sauce, or to
taste

1 teaspoon finely minced fresh ginger

$^{1}/_{2}$ teaspoon dark sesame oil, or to taste

$^{1}/_{8}$ teaspoon ground white pepper, or
to taste

GARNISH (OPTIONAL)   toasted sesame seeds, scallion curls

1. Pour the chicken broth into a large saucepan or Dutch oven; bring to a boil over high heat. Stir in the mushrooms, chicken, carrot, and scallion. When the liquid returns to a boil, reduce the heat to medium; cover and cook for about 10 minutes or until the chicken is cooked through and the vegetables are tender.

2. Stir together the water and cornstarch until smooth in a measuring cup or small bowl. Add the mixture to the soup, stirring constantly until it is clear and thickened. Stir in the soy sauce, ginger, sesame oil, and white pepper. Adjust the seasonings to taste.

PER SERVING: Cal 125/Prot 14.3g/Carb 10.3g/Fat 2.9g/Chol 22mg/Sod 941mg

ADVANCE PREPARATION   Shiitake Mushroom Soup is best served immediately; if necessary, cover and refrigerate for up to 1 day. Reheat, stirring gently, over medium heat.

Variations

- In addition to the carrot and scallion, add up to 1 cup other vegetables, such as shredded spinach leaves, frozen peas, blanched stemmed snow peas, lightly sautéed chopped bok choy, or red bell pepper strips.

- Substitute 1 ounce (1½ cups) dried shiitake mushrooms (see Tips) for the fresh shiitakes.

- Substitute bottled teriyaki sauce for the soy sauce.

TIPS

- Choose plump Shiitake mushrooms with edges that curl under; avoid broken or shriveled caps. Store them in the refrigerator, in a dish covered with a damp paper towel rather than in a closed container. The mushrooms will keep for only 2 or 3 days. Shiitake mushroom stems are extremely tough and therefore should be removed. You can use them to add flavor to stocks and sauces; discard the stems after they have been used for flavoring.

- Dried shiitake mushrooms can be stored at room temperature in a sealed bag or a jar. They must be reconstituted before using: cover them with boiling water and soak for about 5 minutes (or for about 30 minutes in lukewarm water), or until softened. As with fresh shiitake mushrooms, the stems are tough and must be removed.

egg drop
soup

Makes 4 servings

A classic of Chinese cuisine, Egg Drop Soup is simplified here for speedy preparation. If you prefer, cholesterol-free egg substitute works just fine in place of whole eggs.

2 (14^1/2-ounce) cans chicken broth (4 cups)

1 tablespoon low-sodium soy sauce

4 ounces boneless skinless chicken breast halves, cut into 1-inch-long by ^{1}/4-inch-wide strips

1 red bell pepper, cut into 1^1/2-inch-long by ^{1}/8-inch-wide strips

1 cup frozen peas (preferably baby peas); (see Tips)

^{1}/2 cup coarsely shredded carrot

2 medium scallions, minced

1 teaspoon minced garlic

^{1}/4 teaspoon ground white pepper, or to taste

2 eggs (see Tips)

1 teaspoon dark sesame oil, or to taste

GARNISH (OPTIONAL)   toasted sesame seeds

1. Pour the chicken broth into a large saucepan or Dutch oven; stir in the soy sauce. Bring the liquid to a boil over high heat.

2. Stir in the chicken, bell pepper, peas, carrot, scallions, garlic, and white pepper. When the liquid returns to a boil, reduce the heat to medium; cover and cook for about 10 minutes or until the chicken is cooked through and the vegetables are tender.

3. In a measuring cup or small bowl, lightly beat the eggs with a fork until they are light and lemon-colored. Over medium heat, add the eggs to the soup, pouring slowly in a very thin stream; stir constantly until the eggs cook and form shreds. Stir in the sesame oil. Adjust the seasonings to taste.

PER SERVING: Cal 176/Prot 19.2g/Carb 11g/Fat 6.1g/Chol 128mg/Sod 1,005mg

ADVANCE PREPARATION   Egg Drop Soup will keep, covered and refrigerated, for 2 days. Reheat, stirring gently, over medium heat. Better yet, prepare the soup with the chicken and vegetables in advance; add the eggs and sesame oil when reheating just before serving.

Variations

*   Substitute bottled teriyaki sauce for the soy sauce.
*   Substitute $1/2$ cup cholesterol-free egg substitute or 4 egg whites for the eggs (see Tips).

> ## TIPS
>
> *   Although eggs will keep for up to 1 month in the refrigerator, they lose their fresh flavor after 1 week. Store them with the large end up in the coldest part of your refrigerator, not in the molded door rack. Since eggs can absorb odors through their porous shells, storing eggs in the carton helps protect them from the aromas of other foods.
>
> *   Cholesterol-free egg products are made from real egg whites. The flavor is enhanced by the addition of a small amount of corn oil, and some yellow coloring is added to give the appearance of whole eggs. Reduced-cholesterol egg products are made from whole eggs from which nearly all of the cholesterol has been removed.
>
> *   For flavor, baby peas are preferable to standard-size ones; petit pois, or baby peas, harvested when young, remain especially sweet after picking.

soba
noodle
soup

Makes 4 servings

The typical proportions of broth to solid ingredients are reversed in this soup. Here, a large help-
ing of noodles fills the bowls, with the spicy broth, chicken, and vegetables poured over. Make
nothing else for dinner and eat a large bowlful with chopsticks and a Chinese soup spoon.

1 (49$^1/_2$-ounce) can chicken broth (6 cups)

8 ounces boneless skinless chicken breast halves, cut into 2-inch-long by $^1/_2$-inch-wide strips

8 ounces soba (buckwheat) noodles (see Tip)

$^1/_2$ cup coarsely shredded carrot

2 medium scallions, coarsely chopped

1 tablespoon low-sodium soy sauce

1 teaspoon minced garlic

$^1/_2$ teaspoon red pepper flakes, or to taste

$^1/_8$ teaspoon ground white pepper, or to taste

1 teaspoon orange zest

2 tablespoons fresh orange juice

1 teaspoon dark sesame oil, or to taste

GARNISH   coarsely chopped scallions and toasted sesame seeds

1. Pour the chicken broth into a large saucepan or Dutch oven; bring to a boil over high heat.

2. Stir in the chicken, noodles, carrot, scallions, soy sauce, garlic, red pepper flakes, and white pepper. When the liquid returns to a boil, reduce the heat to medium; cover and cook for about 10 minutes or until the chicken is cooked through and the noodles and vegetables are tender.

3. Stir in the orange zest, orange juice, and sesame oil. Adjust the seasonings to taste.

4. To serve, use tongs to fill large soup bowls with the cooked noodles. Arrange chicken strips atop the noodles; pour the broth and vegetables over all.

PER SERVING: Cal 374/Prot 32.8g/Carb 47.8g/Fat 5.7g/Chol 44mg/Sod 1,794mg

ADVANCE PREPARATION   Soba Noodle Soup will keep, covered and refrigerated, for 1 day.

Variations

- Add up to 1 cup other vegetables. Try sliced mushrooms, bok choy (both sliced stalks and shredded greens), frozen peas, or blanched stemmed snow peas.
- With the sesame oil, stir in minced fresh cilantro to taste.

> **TIP**
>
> Soba noodles are Japanese noodles made from buckwheat and wheat flours, giving them a gray-brown color. You'll find them in Asian stores and in the Asian section of most supermarkets.

minestrone
soup

Makes 4 servings

This hearty Italian soup is a contemporary version of my old minestrone soup, which simmered all day. What a pleasant surprise to find that this slim-and-trim soup is equally good with a fraction of the preparation time! Serve with Pita Crisps (page 188) or a loaf of Italian bread, and a robust salad.

1 tablespoon olive oil

1 carrot, cut into 1/8-inch-thick slices

1/4 cup minced onion

1 teaspoon minced garlic

2 (14 1/2-ounce) cans chicken broth (4 cups)

1 (14 1/2-ounce) can diced tomatoes, with juice (see Tip)

1 (14 1/2-ounce) can cannellini beans, drained and rinsed

4 ounces boneless skinless chicken breast halves, cut into 1/2-inch squares

1 medium zucchini, halved lengthwise and cut into 1/4-inch-thick slices

1/2 cup elbow macaroni

2 tablespoons minced fresh basil (or 1/2 teaspoon dried basil)

1 tablespoon minced fresh oregano (or 1/2 teaspoon dried oregano)

1/4 teaspoon pepper, or to taste

GARNISH (OPTIONAL)   freshly ground black pepper, freshly grated Parmesan cheese, Herbed Croutons (page 132)

1. Heat the oil in a large saucepan or Dutch oven over medium-high heat. Add the carrot, onion, and garlic; cook, stirring occasionally, for about 2 minutes or until the carrot is crisp-tender and the onion is translucent and not browned.

2. Stir in the chicken broth and tomatoes with juice; bring to a boil over high heat. Stir in the beans, chicken, zucchini, macaroni, dried basil and oregano (if using), and pepper. When the liquid returns to a boil, reduce the heat to medium; cover and cook for about 10 minutes or until the chicken is cooked through and the pasta and vegetables are tender. Stir in the fresh basil and oregano (if using). Adjust the seasonings to taste.

PER SERVING: Cal 270/Prot 21.7g/Carb 31.1g/Fat 6.5g/Chol 22mg/Sod 973mg

ADVANCE PREPARATION   Minestrone Soup will keep, covered and refrigerated, for up to 2 days.

Variations

- Substitute other beans for the cannellini beans (up to 1²/₃ cups total). Try kidney, pinto, garbanzo, or a combination.

- Add up to 1 cup other vegetables, such as cut green beans or asparagus.

- Add about ¹/₄ cup oil-packed sun-dried tomatoes, drained and coarsely chopped.

- Substitute other pasta for the macaroni, such as small shells or spaghetti broken into 2-inch lengths.

- Omit the basil and oregano and flavor the soup with about 2 tablespoons Basil Pesto (page 97), or to taste.

> **TIP**
>
> When buying canned tomatoes, read the labels. Some tomatoes are canned whole. Others are diced (recipe-ready tomatoes); select these for recipes calling for canned chopped tomatoes. Other canned tomatoes contain herbs and seasonings, such as stewed tomatoes. Plum tomatoes are sold as "Italian" tomatoes. In cooked recipes, canned tomatoes are usually preferable to fresh tomatoes of poor quality.

black bean
soup

Makes 4 servings

Most often, cream is the thickening element in soups; here, puréed beans provide the texture. The result is a bean soup with plenty of body, flavor, nutrients—and lower fat. Jalapeño pepper and cumin lend the soup a zesty flavor; adjust the amounts to suit your taste. As a garnish or accompaniment, serve Chili Tortilla Strips (page 190).

2 tablespoons olive oil, divided

8 ounces boneless skinless chicken breast halves, cut into $1/2$-inch squares

1 rib celery, finely chopped

$1/4$ cup finely chopped onion

2 teaspoons minced fresh jalapeño pepper, seeds removed (see Tip)

1 teaspoon minced garlic

1 ($14^{1}/2$-ounce) can chicken broth (2 cups)

1 ($14^{1}/2$-ounce) can diced tomatoes, with juice

1 (15-ounce) can black beans, drained and rinsed

1 teaspoon ground cumin

$1/2$ teaspoon pepper, or to taste

1 tablespoon minced fresh cilantro, or to taste (do not substitute dried cilantro; if fresh is unavailable, substitute 1 tablespoon minced fresh basil or oregano or

1 teaspoon dried basil or oregano)

GARNISH (OPTIONAL)   dollops of plain yogurt, diced red bell peppers, sprigs of fresh cilantro

1.   Heat 1 tablespoon of the oil in a large saucepan or Dutch oven over medium-high heat. Add the chicken; cook, stirring occasionally for about 5 minutes or until it is cooked through and lightly browned.

2. With a slotted spoon, transfer the chicken to a bowl and cover to keep warm.

3. Heat the remaining 1 tablespoon of oil in the pan. Add the celery and onion; cook, stirring occasionally, for about 5 minutes. Add the jalapeño pepper and garlic; continue to cook, stirring constantly, for about 1 more minute or until the vegetables are tender.

4. Stir in the chicken broth, tomatoes with juice, beans, cumin, pepper, and dried basil or oregano (if using).

5. Remove about half of the soup mixture; process in a food processor or blender until smooth. Pour back into the pan; stir in the cooked chicken and fresh cilantro (if using). Heat, stirring occasionally. Adjust the seasoning to taste.

PER SERVING: Cal 339/Prot 29.6g/Carb 32.3g/Fat 10.1g/Chol 44mg/Sod 628mg

ADVANCE PREPARATION   Black Bean Soup will keep, covered and refrigerated, for up to 2 days. Add water as necessary when reheating.

Variation

- For a milder flavor, substitute 1 tablespoon minced Anaheim pepper or 1 tablespoon canned diced green chilies for the fresh jalapeño pepper.

> **TIP**
>
> Jalapeños, one of the most familiar chili peppers, are small, smooth-skinned green peppers (scarlet when ripe) about 2 inches in length. They are readily available in most markets, both fresh and canned. Those in cans or jars are milder than fresh because they are peeled, seeded, and packed in liquid. Store fresh peppers in a plastic bag in your refrigerator, where they will keep for about 1 week.

chicken
chili
with raisins

Makes 4 servings

Often I make a double batch of this chili, because I love having leftovers! For variety, mound warm chili over split baked potatoes, and pop them under the broiler to melt a topping of Parmesan cheese.

2 tablespoons olive oil, divided

8 ounces boneless skinless chicken breast halves, cut into 1-inch pieces

1/2 cup coarsely chopped onion

1 green bell pepper, coarsely chopped

2 ribs celery, coarsely chopped

1 teaspoon minced garlic

1 (18-ounce) can whole tomatoes, with juice

1 (15-ounce) can kidney beans, drained and rinsed

1 (15-ounce) can tomato sauce

1 (9-ounce) package frozen corn (1 1/2 cups), thawed

2 teaspoons chili powder, or to taste

3 drops hot pepper sauce, or to taste (see Tip)

1 teaspoon ground cumin

1 teaspoon dried basil

1 teaspoon dried oregano

1/2 teaspoon pepper, or to taste

1/2 cup raisins

GARNISH (OPTIONAL)   coarsely chopped scallions, Baked Tortilla Chips (page 187), shredded Monterey Jack or Cheddar cheese

1. Heat 1 tablespoon of the olive oil in a large saucepan or Dutch oven over medium-high heat. Add the chicken; cook, stirring occasionally, for about 5 minutes or until it is lightly browned and cooked through.

2. With a slotted spoon, transfer the chicken to a bowl and cover to keep warm.

3. Heat the remaining 1 tablespoon of oil in the pan. Add the onion, bell pepper, and celery; cook, stirring occasionally, for about 5 minutes. Add the garlic; continue to stir constantly for about 1 minute or until the vegetables are crisp-tender.

4. Stir in the tomatoes with juice, beans, tomato sauce, corn, chili powder, hot pepper sauce, cumin, basil, oregano, and pepper. Increase the heat to high and bring the mixture to a boil.

5. Stir in the cooked chicken and raisins; heat through. Adjust the seasonings to taste.

PER SERVING: Cal 434/Prot 28.3g/Carb 58.5g/Fat 9.7g/Chol 44mg/Sod 673mg

ADVANCE PREPARATION   Chicken Chili with Raisins will keep, covered and refrigerated for up to 2 days. The flavors will blend, and the dish reheats well. If necessary, add extra liquid when reheating; use water, vegetable stock, or tomato juice.

Variations

*   While cooking the onion, add other vegetables, such as 1 cup sliced mushrooms or zucchini or 1 seeded and chopped jalapeño pepper; or, when stirring in the tomatoes, add up to 1 cup cubed potato and/or about 1/4 cup diced green chilies.

*   Substitute other beans for kidney beans. Try pinto, garbanzo, black beans, or a combination (about 1 2/3 cups total).

*   For a hotter chili, add a dash of cayenne pepper or a pinch of red pepper flakes.

> **TIP**
>
> Once opened, refrigerate hot pepper sauce to retain its flavor and color.

Mexican Taco Soup

mexican
taco
soup

Makes 4 servings

Who doesn't love tacos? This zesty soup corrals all those favorite flavors. Add a minced fresh jalapeño pepper and a few drops of hot pepper sauce or a pinch of red pepper flakes if you like your Mexican food more spirited. As a garnish or accompaniment, serve Baked Tortilla Chips (page 187).

1 tablespoon olive oil

8 ounces boneless skinless chicken breast halves, cut into 1-inch-long by $1/2$-inch-wide strips

$1/2$ red bell pepper, coarsely chopped

1 rib celery, coarsely chopped (also shred green tops)

$1/4$ cup coarsely chopped onion

2 teaspoons minced garlic

1 ($10^1/2$-ounce) can chicken broth ($1^1/4$ cups)

1 ($14^1/2$-ounce) can diced tomatoes, with juice

1 ($14^1/2$-ounce) can garbanzo beans, drained and rinsed (see Tip)

1 (4-ounce) can diced green chilies, drained

$1/2$ cup frozen corn

$1/2$ teaspoon ground cumin

$1/2$ teaspoon pepper, or to taste

2 tablespoons minced fresh flat-leaf parsley

1 tablespoon minced fresh cilantro, or to taste (do not substitute dried cilantro; if fresh is unavailable, substitute 1 tablespoon minced fresh basil or oregano or 1 teaspoon dried basil or oregano)

GARNISH (OPTIONAL)   sprigs of fresh cilantro, shredded Cheddar or Monterey Jack cheese, Baked Tortilla Chips (page 187)

(continues)

185

1. Heat the oil in a large saucepan or Dutch oven over medium-high heat. Add the chicken; cook, stirring occasionally, for about 3 minutes or until it is lightly browned but not cooked through. Stir in the bell pepper, celery, onion, and garlic. Cook, stirring occasionally, for about 5 minutes or until the chicken is cooked through and the vegetables are tender.

2. Stir in the chicken broth, tomatoes with juice, beans, green chilies, corn, cumin, pepper, and dried basil or oregano (if using). Increase the heat to high; when the mixture comes to a boil, reduce the heat to medium; cover and cook for 5 minutes. Stir in the parsley and fresh cilantro (if using) during the last minute or two. Adjust the seasoning to taste.

PER SERVING: Calories 288/Prot 25.1g/Carb 29.2g/Fat 7.9g/Chol 44mg/Sod 1,281mg

ADVANCE PREPARATION   Mexican Taco Soup will keep, covered and refrigerated, for up to 2 days. The flavors will blend, and the soup reheats well.

Variation

- Substitute other beans for the garbanzo beans (up to $1^2/_3$ cups total). Try black beans, pinto beans, kidney beans, or a combination.

TIP

Garbanzo beans are sometimes called chickpeas, ceci beans, or Spanish beans. They are nutlike in flavor—and nutlike in appearance, too, for they are shaped like a hazelnut. Cooking garbanzo beans from scratch requires about 8 hours of soaking and 3 hours of cooking. Canned garbanzo beans are a great alternative for the 15-minute cook, drain and rinse.

baked
tortilla
chips

Makes 4 servings (6 chips per serving)

These delicious chips are a low-fat alternative to the packaged varieties, which seem to be high in fat and salt or short on flavor. White-flour tortillas toast better than whole wheat ones. I use these as a soup accompaniment, but they also can be served with salsas or dips as a snack or appetizer.

4 (6- or 7-inch) flour tortillas

1. Preheat the oven to 400°F.

2. With kitchen shears, cut each tortilla into 6 wedges. Arrange them in a single layer on an ungreased baking sheet.

3. Bake for about 5 to 7 minutes or until the chips are lightly browned and crisp. (The chips will become crisper as they cool.)

PER SERVING: Cal 95/Prot 2.5g/Carb 17.3g/Fat 1.8g/Chol 0mg/Sod 110mg

ADVANCE PREPARATION   Baked Tortilla Chips can be made in advance and stored in an airtight container at room temperature for a few days, but they are best if served immediately after baking.

Variations

*   Lightly brush each side of the tortilla with about 1/2 teaspoon olive oil before cutting into wedges.
*   Rather than cutting into wedges, cut the tortillas into 2-inch-long by 1/4-inch-wide strips.

187

pita crisps

Makes 4 servings (6 Pita Crisps per serving)

As a crispy accompaniment to soups or salads, Pita Crisps are my choice. Keep a package of pita bread in the refrigerator or freezer, ready to top and pop in the oven.

2 (6-inch) pita breads (white or whole wheat), each sliced in half horizontally (see Tip)

1 tablespoon olive oil

1 teaspoon dried oregano

1/4 cup freshly grated Parmesan cheese

1. Position the oven rack 4 to 5 inches from the broiling element. Preheat the broiler.

2. With a pastry brush, spread the rough sides of each pita half with olive oil. Place on a baking sheet, oiled sides up; sprinkle with the oregano and Parmesan cheese. Use kitchen shears to cut each pita half into 6 wedges.

3. Broil for about 2 minutes or until the pita wedges are lightly browned and the cheese is melted. Watch closely! The Pita Crisps will continue to become crisp as they cool.

PER SERVING: Cal 128/Prot 6.6g/Carb 10.5g/Fat 6.6g/Chol 5mg/Sod 224mg

ADVANCE PREPARATION   Pita Crisps are best if prepared just before serving. If you have extras, store for a day or two in a tin rather than in a plastic container. They can be made crisp again by heating them on a baking sheet for about 5 minutes at 350°F.

Variations

- Substitute other dried herbs for the oregano. Try basil, rosemary, or thyme.

- Omit the herbs and sprinkle with sesame seeds.

- Rather than cutting the pitas into wedges, cut into $1/2$- or 1-inch-wide strips.

> **TIP**
>
> The flatness of pita or "pocket" bread may make you think it is unleavened, but it is made with yeast. The rounds of dough puff up during baking and then deflate, leaving a hollow in the middle.

chili
tortilla
strips

Makes 4 servings

These crunchy chips are ideal with soup. Sometimes I double the recipe to have extras on hand for snacking.

4 (6- or 7-inch) flour tortillas

2 teaspoons olive oil

1 teaspoon chili powder (see Tip)

1/4 teaspoon ground cumin

TIP

In Mexican markets, chili powder is simply a powdered form of ancho, pasilla, or other dried red peppers. The domestic varieties usually contain chili pepper with extra seasonings, such as cumin, oregano, garlic, black pepper, and paprika. If you want to make your chili powder hotter, add cayenne pepper.

1. Preheat the oven to 400°F.

2. Lightly brush both sides of each tortilla with the oil. With kitchen shears, cut the tortillas into 1-inch-wide strips. Place them in a single layer on an ungreased baking sheet.

3. Combine the chili powder and cumin in a small bowl; sprinkle over the strips.

4. Bake for about 5 minutes or until the strips are lightly browned and crisp. (The strips will become crisper as they cool.)

PER SERVING: Cal 119/Prot 2.6g/Carb 17.7g/Fat 4.2g/Chol 0mg/Sod 7mg

ADVANCE PREPARATION   Chili Tortilla Strips can be made in advance and stored in an airtight container at room temperature for a few days, but they are best if served immediately after baking.

chapter 5

Chicken Sandwiches
and Pizzas

A CHICKEN SANDWICH CAN BE MUCH MORE THAN THE

obvious sliced chicken between two pieces of bread. If you

are bored, consider the many possibilities for international

variety using Italian, Asian, Mexican, or Southwestern inspi-

rations. The chicken itself can be sautéed, broiled, or grilled;

the breasts can be used whole, sliced, or even ground

and formed into chicken burgers or pâté to be used as a

sandwich spread. Expand your image of the sandwich beyond bread, too; tortillas and pita bread pockets make interesting packages and are delicious in their own right.

Pizza, anyone? With tortillas as crusts, chicken pizzas can be on the table even faster than the delivery service can have them at your door. These are not ordinary pizzas either; the possibilities for gourmet variations are as endless as your sense of adventure.

These recipes are excellent choices for lunch or a light dinner. Simply add a salad—and applause!

lemon-basil chicken
in **pita bread**
pockets

Makes 4 servings

*Accompanied by a light salad, this dish makes an appealing summer lunch. And it can be
prepared in about 10 minutes! For variety, grill or broil the chicken (see methods on page 62).*

4 boneless skinless chicken breast halves
(about 4 ounces each)

1 tablespoon olive oil

12 large fresh basil leaves (do not substitute dried basil; if fresh is unavailable,
substitute fresh stemmed salad spinach
leaves)

4 (6-inch) pita breads (white or whole
wheat), each sliced in half vertically

8 leaves soft leaf lettuce (such as Bibb,
Boston, green leaf, or red leaf)

Chutney-Yogurt Sauce

$^1/_3$ cup low-fat plain yogurt

3 tablespoons mango chutney

2 tablespoons fresh lemon juice

1 teaspoon grated lemon rind

1. Place the chicken breasts between 2 sheets of plastic wrap or place in a plastic bag;
flatten them to a $^1/_2$-inch uniform thickness.

2. Heat the oil in a large nonstick skillet over medium-high heat. Add the chicken
breasts; cook for about 4 minutes on each side or until they are lightly browned and
cooked through.

3. With a slotted spatula, transfer the chicken to a plate and cover to keep warm.

(continues)

4. Stir together the sauce ingredients in a small bowl. Spread about 1 tablespoon of the sauce on one side of each chicken breast; arrange 3 basil leaves on top. Slice the chicken breasts in half.

5. For each sandwich, open 2 pita bread pockets; line each with lettuce leaves. Slip in the chicken breast pieces. Drizzle each half with about 2 teaspoons of the sauce.

PER SERVING: Cal 342/Prot 37.9g/Carb 30.2g/Fat 7.7g/Chol 88mg/Sod 302mg

ADVANCE PREPARATION   The chicken can be cooked up to 1 day in advance, refrigerated, and served chilled. The sauce can be prepared up to 1 day ahead. Assemble the pita sandwiches just before serving.

Variations

• Substitute reduced-fat, cholesterol-free mayonnaise for the yogurt.

• Cut the cooked chicken into cubes; toss with the Chutney-Yogurt Sauce, and stuff into pita bread pockets or serve on a bed of greens as a warm or chilled chicken salad.

Lemon-Basil Chicken in Pita Bread Pockets

blackened
chicken
pitas

Makes 4 servings

Garnish the plates with large bunches of seedless red grapes or fresh orange wedges.

Seasoning Mixture

3 tablespoons extra-virgin olive oil

1 tablespoon minced garlic

1 teaspoon paprika

$1/2$ teaspoon pepper

$1/4$ teaspoon cayenne pepper

$1/4$ teaspoon ground cumin

$1/8$ teaspoon salt

To Complete the Recipe

$1/2$ cup low-fat plain yogurt

$1/2$ teaspoon sugar

4 boneless skinless chicken breast halves
(about 4 ounces each)

2 (6-inch) pita breads (white or whole
wheat), each sliced in half vertically

8 leaves soft leaf lettuce; such as Bibb,
Boston, green leaf, or red leaf (see Tip)

1. Stir together the seasoning mixture in a small bowl.

2. Pour the yogurt into a separate small bowl. Add 2 teaspoons of the seasoning mixture and the sugar; stir until the sugar is dissolved. Set aside.

3. Place the chicken breasts between 2 sheets of plastic wrap or place in a plastic bag; flatten them to a $1/2$-inch uniform thickness. Spread the seasoning mixture on both sides of each chicken breast.

4. Heat a stovetop grill pan over high heat. Reduce the heat to medium-high and arrange the chicken on the grill; cook for about 4 minutes. Turn the chicken and cook for about 4 more minutes or until it is well browned (and somewhat blackened) and cooked through.

5. Transfer the chicken to a plate.

6. Spread about 1 tablespoon of the yogurt mixture on the top of each chicken breast. Slice the chicken breasts in half.

7. For each sandwich, open 2 pita bread pockets; line each with lettuce leaves. Slip in the chicken breast halves. Drizzle each sandwich with about 1 more tablespoon of the yogurt mixture.

PER SERVING: Cal 390/Prot 38.9g/Carb 25.5g/Fat 14.7g/Chol 89mg/Sod 375mg

ADVANCE PREPARATION   The yogurt sauce can be made several hours in advance; cover and refrigerate. The chicken breasts can be spread with the seasoning mixture, placed in a single layer on a plate, covered with plastic wrap, and refrigerated for several hours before cooking. If you prefer, the chicken can be cooked up to 1 day in advance and served chilled. Assemble the pita sandwiches just before serving.

Variations

- Cut the cooked chicken into cubes; toss with the yogurt sauce, and stuff into pita bread pockets or serve on a bed of greens as a warm or chilled salad.

- Slice the cooked chicken into thin diagonal strips; serve on a bed of greens tossed with Southwestern Vinaigrette (page 118) or Herbed Tomato Vinaigrette (page 197).

TIP

Boston lettuce (sometimes called butterhead lettuce) is a small, round, loosely formed head with soft, buttery-textured leaves ranging from pale green to pale yellow-green. The flavor is sweet, and the leaves are tender and fragile. Bibb lettuce is another variety in the butterhead family. Loose-leaf lettuces are those varieties that don't form heads but consist of large, loosely packed leaves joined at a stem. Their crispness is somewhere between that of romaine and butterhead; their taste is mild and delicate. Oak leaf, red leaf, and green leaf are some popular varieties.

italian
chicken
and **vegetable sandwiches**

Makes 4 servings

This sandwich filling is a natural to bundle in a pita bread pocket; or, for variety, serve the filling in a bowl for spooning onto toasted Italian bread slices.

Italian Dressing

1/4 cup white wine vinegar

1/4 cup drained and minced oil-packed
  sun-dried tomatoes

2 tablespoons extra-virgin olive oil

1 teaspoon minced shallot

1 teaspoon minced fresh flat-leaf parsley

1 teaspoon minced fresh oregano (or
  1/4 teaspoon dried oregano)

1/4 teaspoon pepper, or to taste

Pinch of red pepper flakes, or to taste

Pinch of powdered mustard

To Complete the Recipe

1 tablespoon olive oil

1 pound boneless skinless chicken breast
  halves, cut into 2-inch-long by
  1/2-inch-wide strips

1 red bell pepper, cut into 2-inch by 1/4-
  inch strips

4 (6-inch) pita breads (white or whole
  wheat), each sliced in half vertically

8 leaves soft leaf lettuce (green leaf or
  red leaf)

GARNISH (OPTIONAL)   freshly ground black pepper, crumbled feta cheese (see Tip), or chèvre cheese

1. Whisk together the dressing ingredients in a small bowl or measuring cup. Adjust the seasonings to taste. Set aside.

2. Heat the oil in a large skillet over medium-high heat. Add the chicken; cook, stirring occasionally, for about 2 to 3 minutes or until it is no longer pink on the outside. Add the bell pepper; continue to cook, stirring occasionally, for about 2 minutes.

3. Reduce the heat to low. Whisk the dressing; stir it into the chicken-vegetable mixture. Cover and cook for about 3 minutes or until the bell pepper is crisp-tender and the chicken is cooked through.

4. Line each pita bread pocket with a lettuce leaf; spoon the chicken filling into the pocket.

> **PER SERVING:** Cal 414/Prot 38.8g/Carb 32.6g/Fat 14.3g/Chol 87mg/Sod 304mg

ADVANCE PREPARATION   If dried oregano is used, the Italian dressing will keep for up to 1 week in a tightly closed container in the refrigerator; if fresh oregano is used, the dressing will keep for up to 4 days. The chicken and vegetable mixture can be cooked early on the day it is to be served; cover and refrigerate. Assemble the sandwiches just before serving.

Variation

- Substitute other vegetables for all or part of the red bell pepper (up to 1½ cups total). Try strips of green or yellow bell pepper, strips of zucchini, or sliced mushrooms.

TIP

Feta cheese is a white Greek cheese with a rich, tangy flavor. Traditionally, it is made with goat's milk, sheep's milk, or a combination; today it is also often made with cow's milk. Fresh feta is crumbly with whey; when mature, it becomes drier and saltier.

chicken tortilla sandwiches
with **jalapeño**
mayonnaise

Makes 4 servings

When time is short but you want to serve something unusual for lunch, here's a sensational warm chicken sandwich to make folks sit up and take notice. Juicy fruit adds a nice balance to the spiciness of the jalapeño mayonnaise.

Jalapeño Mayonnaise

$1/3$ cup reduced-fat cholesterol-free mayonnaise (see Tip)

1 plum tomato, diced (about $1/2$ cup)

1 tablespoon minced jalapeño pepper, or to taste

1 medium scallion, minced

1 teaspoon fresh lime juice

Dash of pepper, or to taste

To Complete the Recipe

2 boneless skinless chicken breast halves (about 4 ounces each)

2 teaspoons olive oil, divided

Dash of pepper, or to taste

4 (6- or 7-inch) flour tortillas (white or whole wheat)

8 leaves soft leaf lettuce (such as Bibb, Boston, green leaf, or red leaf)

4 toothpicks

GARNISH (OPTIONAL)   fresh fruit, such as orange wedges

1. To prepare the jalapeño mayonnaise, stir together the ingredients in a small bowl. Adjust the seasoning to taste. Set aside.

2. Place the chicken breasts between 2 sheets of plastic wrap or place in a plastic bag; flatten them to a uniform $1/4$-inch thickness.

3. Heat a stovetop grill pan over high heat. Brush one side of each chicken breast with about half of the oil. Reduce the heat to medium-high and arrange the chicken on the grill, oiled sides down; cook for about 4 minutes. Brush the top surfaces with the remaining oil; turn and continue to cook for about 3 minutes or until the chicken is lightly browned and cooked through.

4. Transfer the chicken to a plate and sprinkle with pepper. Slice the chicken into $1/4$-inch-wide strips; cover to keep warm.

5. Place the tortillas between 2 paper towels. Microwave for about 15 to 20 seconds or until they are moist and warm. (Or wrap the tortillas in aluminum foil and heat in a preheated 350°F oven for about 10 minutes.)

6. Spread each tortilla with about 3 tablespoons of the Jalapeño Mayonnaise; top with a layer of lettuce. Place the chicken strips across the center of each tortilla. Fold the edges over the chicken, overlapping them at the center. Fasten each with a toothpick.

> **TIP**
>
> Mayonnaise, an emulsified sauce traditionally based on egg yolks, comes in several variations. Reduced-fat cholesterol-free mayonnaise (with 25 to 50 percent less fat than regular mayonnaise) and nonfat mayonnaise are available in most supermarkets. Refrigerated, commercially prepared mayonnaise will keep for up to 6 months.

PER SERVING: Cal 253/Prot 19.3g/Carb 22.3g/Fat 9.6g/Chol 44mg/Sod 69mg

ADVANCE PREPARATION   The Jalapeño Mayonnaise can be made up to 1 day in advance. Prepare the chicken just before serving.

Variation

• Cut the cooked chicken into 1-inch squares and toss with the Jalapeño Mayonnaise; serve on beds of lettuce or stuff the chicken mixture into pita bread pockets.

italian
chicken
burgers

Serve these burgers on toasted buns or slices of Italian bread with tomato slices and lettuce. Accompany with Corn and Rice Salad (page 93).

1 pound boneless skinless chicken breast halves, ground

$^1/_2$ cup cooked rice (white or brown)

1 tablespoon minced fresh basil (or 1 teaspoon dried basil)

2 tablespoons tomato paste

1 tablespoon minced onion

$^1/_2$ teaspoon minced garlic

$^1/_2$ teaspoon pepper

Dash of salt

Follow the procedure below to make the burgers.

PER SERVING: Cal 239/Prot 34g/Carb 10g/Fat 7g/Chol 87mg/Sod 110mg

MAKING CHICKEN BURGERS

Where's the beef? Well, who cares? Nobody will, when these juicy, flavorful chicken burgers are on the menu. The seasonings give each burger a totally different personality. Each recipe makes 4 servings.

1. Some supermarkets sell ground chicken, but it takes only seconds to produce at home. To grind the chicken, quarter the raw boneless skinless breast halves; drop into the bowl of a food processor fitted with a steel blade. Process by pulsing with the on-off button to chop—the chicken will be ready in a flash.

2. Transfer the ground chicken to a medium mixing bowl; stir in the remaining ingredients. Form each mixture into 4 patties, each 4 inches in diameter and about $^1/_2$ inch thick.

3. Heat the oil in a medium nonstick skillet over medium-high heat. Add the patties and cook for about 5 minutes on each side or until they are lightly browned and cooked through. (If you prefer, the burgers can be broiled or cooked on either a stovetop grill pan or outdoor grill.)

4. Serve the patties on frills of leaf lettuce or on toasted buns (I prefer whole wheat) with your choice of accompaniments.

mexican
chicken
burgers

Serve these burgers on toasted buns with tomato slices and lettuce; drizzle with taco sauce. Accompany with Tomato-Corn Salsa (page 92).

1 pound boneless skinless chicken breast halves, ground

^{1}/$_2$ cup cooked rice (white or brown)

^{1}/$_4$ cup cooked black beans (drain and rinse canned beans)

2 tablespoons tomato paste

1 tablespoon minced onion

1 teaspoon chili powder

^{1}/$_2$ teaspoon minced garlic

^{1}/$_2$ teaspoon pepper

Dash of salt

Follow the procedure on page 202 to make the burgers.

PER SERVING: Cal 253/Prot 35g/Carb 12.2g/Fat 7.1g/Chol 87mg/Sod 116mg

Variation

• Substitute other beans for the black beans. Try kidney beans or garbanzo beans.

chicken-mushroom pâté

Makes 4 servings

Serve this pâté warm or at room temperature with thick slabs of country-style bread; toasted, thinly sliced whole wheat or rye bread; or unsalted crackers. It makes a terrific appetizer; but most often, I enjoy this as a spread for open-faced sandwiches.

1 (10$^{1}/_{2}$-ounce) can chicken broth (1$^{1}/_{4}$ cups)

Water, if necessary

1 carrot, sliced

2 sprigs fresh flat-leaf parsley

1 bay leaf

8 ounces boneless skinless chicken breast halves

1 tablespoon olive oil

2 cups sliced mushrooms (preferably cremini)

2 tablespoons finely chopped onion (see Tip)

1 teaspoon minced garlic

$^{1}/_{2}$ teaspoon dried tarragon

2 tablespoons low-sodium soy sauce

1 tablespoon fresh lemon juice

$^{1}/_{4}$ teaspoon ground white pepper, or to taste

GARNISH (OPTIONAL) sprigs of fresh flat-leaf parsley, halved cherry tomatoes

1. To poach the chicken breasts, pour the chicken broth into a small sauté pan; add enough water so that the liquid is about 1$^{1}/_{2}$ inches deep. Add the carrot, parsley, and bay leaf. Bring the liquid to a boil over high heat. Add the chicken (it should be covered by about $^{1}/_{2}$ inch broth mixture); reduce the heat to medium. Cover and cook for about 8 to 10 minutes or until the chicken is just cooked through.

2. With a slotted spoon, remove the chicken from the sauté pan; quarter the breasts and transfer to the bowl of a food processor fitted with a steel blade. Add the carrot. (Discard the parsley, bay leaf, and poaching liquid.)

3. Meanwhile, heat the oil in a medium nonstick skillet over medium-high heat. Add the mushrooms, onion, and garlic; cook, stirring occasionally, for about 3 minutes or until the mushrooms and onion are tender but not browned. Stir in the tarragon.

4. Pour the mushroom mixture into the food processor with the chicken and carrot; add the soy sauce, lemon juice, and white pepper. Process until the mixture is smooth. Adjust the seasoning to taste.

PER SERVING: Cal 134/Prot 18g/Carb 3.6g/Fat 5.3g/Chol 44mg/Sod 315mg

ADVANCE PREPARATION   Chicken Mushroom Pâté can be served warm or at room temperature shortly after preparing, but it actually improves in flavor if it is refrigerated overnight. Bring to room temperature before serving.

Variation

• Use other seasonings, such as basil, oregano, dill, or curry powder.

> **TIP**
>
> When you need only part of an onion, do not peel it before cutting. The unused portion will keep better in the refrigerator if the skin is left on. Wrap it tightly in plastic wrap or store it in a screw-top jar. Or, if you prefer, chop leftover onion and store it in a refrigerator container or a zip-top plastic bag. Frozen in a plastic bag, chopped onion will keep for months. Refrigerated onions do not release tear-producing vapors as readily as those stored at room temperature. To remove onion odor, rub your hands with salt, vinegar, or lemon juice, rinse with cold water, and then wash with warm water and soap.

chapter **5** *Chicken Sandwiches and Pizzas*

mexican
tortilla
pizzas

Makes 4 servings (one 6-inch pizza)

Pizza crusts made from toasted tortillas are quick to prepare and deliciously crispy in texture. They are an ideal base for a wide variety of toppings.

1 boneless skinless chicken breast half (about 4 ounces)

4 teaspoons olive oil, divided

4 (6- or 7-inch) flour tortillas (white flour toasts better than whole wheat)

1/2 cup bottled taco sauce

1/2 cup oil-packed sun-dried tomatoes, drained and coarsely chopped

1 tablespoon minced fresh oregano (or 1 teaspoon dried oregano)

1/4 cup chèvre cheese (see Tip)

1/4 cup freshly grated Parmesan cheese

1. Position the oven rack to 4 to 5 inches from the heating element; preheat the broiler.

2. Heat a stovetop grill pan over high heat. Brush one side of the chicken breast with about 1 teaspoon of the oil. Reduce the heat to medium-high and place the chicken breast on the grill, oiled side down. Cook for about 5 minutes. Brush the top surface with about 1 teaspoon of oil; turn and continue to cook for about 5 minutes or until the chicken is lightly browned and thoroughly cooked.

3. While the chicken is cooking, brush both sides of each tortilla with oil, using about 1/4 teaspoon on each side. Prick the surface of the tortillas in several places with a fork. Place the tortillas directly on the oven rack; broil for about 1 to 2 minutes on each side or until lightly browned. Watch closely!

4. Place the tortillas on a baking sheet. Spread the surface of each with the taco sauce. Cut the cooked chicken into $1/2$-inch squares. Divide the chicken and sun-dried tomatoes and arrange atop the taco sauce. Sprinkle each pizza with dried oregano (if using), dot with the chèvre cheese, and sprinkle with the Parmesan cheese.

5. Broil for about $1^{1}/2$ to 2 minutes, or just until the cheeses melt. Watch closely! If using fresh basil, sprinkle atop each pizza after broiling.

PER SERVING: Cal 360/Prot 20g/Carb 39.5g/Fat 13.6g/Chol 42mg/Sod 370mg

ADVANCE PREPARATION   The tortillas can be toasted early on the day the pizzas are to be served; set aside at room temperature (this is not recommended if the weather is humid, because the tortillas will lose their crispiness). Assemble and broil the pizzas just before serving.

> ### TIP
> Chèvre and Montrachet are tangy, mild, and creamy cheeses made from goat's milk. Domestic goat cheese is a fine substitute for the more expensive, imported brands. Once opened, wrap tightly in plastic wrap; store it in the refrigerator for 1 to 2 weeks. Do not confuse chèvre with caprini, Italian goat cheese, which is dried, less creamy, and more acidic.

Variations

- Substitute 2 pita breads (whole wheat or white) for the tortillas. Slice each horizontally into 2 rounds; brush the rough sides with a little olive oil and broil for about 2 minutes to toast.

- For additional toppings, try canned, diced green chilies, thin onion slices, corn, or black or kidney beans.

- Substitute dried basil for the oregano before broiling, or sprinkle with minced fresh cilantro after broiling.

- Substitute other cheeses for the Parmesan cheese. Try shredded Cheddar or Monterey Jack cheese.

- For Italian pizzas, substitute tomato paste for the taco sauce and basil for the oregano; add a layer of sliced plum tomatoes atop the tomato paste.

index

Page numbers in *italics* refer to illustrations.